THE
BLESSING

How to Quickly Receive

The Blessing

From God

JIM KIBLER

All Scriptures quotations are from
the King James Version or Paraphrased.

The Blessing
Copyright © 2013 Jim Kibler
ISBN: 1492148407
ISBN 13: 9781492148401
Library of Congress Control Number: 2013915367
CreateSpace Independent Publishing Platform
North Charleston, South Carolina

ACKNOWLEDGEMENTS

Mary Kibler, my wife and ministry partner for her suggestions, editing and support.

Jean Johnson, for her suggestions, editing and prayers.

All of God's people, who know that the **first step** to receiving The Blessing of Abraham is to Receive Jesus as your Savior.

If you have never done so just pray this prayer, with all of your heart and you will be saved for all eternity.

Heavenly Father, I repent for all of my sins and I believe Jesus is the Son of God and He rose from the dead after suffering for my sins. I receive you now, Lord Jesus, into my heart and I will serve you for all of eternity.

If you just prayed this prayer you will spend all eternity with Jesus.

All Scriptures quotations are from the King James Version or Paraphrased.

CONTENTS

Preface vii

Introduction xi

Chapter 1 Nothing Else Matters but The Blessing. 1

Chapter 2 The Curse of the Law and Redemption. 37

Chapter 3 The Spoken Blessing. 75

Chapter 4 The Blessing Connector. 107

Chapter 5 Faith To Receive The Blessing of Abraham 119

Chapter 6 The Throne of Grace 145

            167 Scriptural Facts About The Blessing 157

            About The Author 183

PREFACE

The Same Exact Blessing that was on Abraham is upon you, if you are born again. It is what God Intended for you to have when He spoke The Blessing over Adam and Eve in the Garden of Eden.

In order for the Blessing of Abraham to be manifested in the life of a person it must be received by faith. Everything God has provided by grace, through Jesus, must be possessed by faith. This includes salvation, as well as healing.

People are living with sickness, lack and failure because they have not received the Blessing that has already been provided for them.

This Book will take you from the Cross, where Jesus paid for our Redemption, to The Throne of Grace, where you will Receive Grace, by faith, to live in the Fullness of The Blessing of Abraham.

Every time you see the words, Bless, Blessing, or Blessed, in the Bible, the writers are referring to the same Blessing that God spoke over Adam and Eve, Noah and his Sons, Abraham, Isaac and Jacob.

This Book is designed to quickly bring the Blessing of Abraham, which belongs to you and is your inheritance, into your life.

There are two things that you, as a Christian, must know:

1. What God has already given to you.

2. How to possess it.

This Book is going to teach you how to quickly begin to live your life in The Blessing of Abraham. And also, how to get The Curse of The Law, which is destroying the lives of God's people, out of your life forever.

Read this book over and over again and even read it out loud, until the words have been planted into your heart and you are living in the fullness of The Blessing. It will not take as long as you might think to receive The Blessing.

Be a Blessing to others and get a copy of this book for everyone in your family. Tell your friends and people in your church about this book, so that they may also live in The Fullness of The Blessing of Abraham.

Give your Pastor a copy of this book and watch The Blessing come into your church.

It is time that God's people walk in the inheritance that belongs to them.

As you read this book, your whole life will change.

Pray this prayer over yourself every day that the Apostle Paul prayed over the Ephesians and God will give you incredible revelation knowledge of His Word.

That the God of our Lord Jesus Christ, the Father of Glory, may give unto me the spirit of wisdom and revelation in the knowledge of Him. That the eyes of my understanding would be enlightened; that I may know what is the hope of His calling, and the riches of the glory of His inheritance for the Saints. Amen.

Go to **www.increasenow.com** and listen to Pastor Jim's <u>**Free Sermons**</u> on Increase, Redemption and living in The Blessing of Abraham.

Please Share your praise reports at Jkibler100@aol.com

<u>The Blessing Movement is coming.</u>

Be a part of it and live your life in the Fullness of The Blessing of God.

May God Bless you as you read this book and may The Blessing of Abraham come upon you and the entire Body of Christ.

Pastor Jim Kibler

INTRODUCTION

People don't know what they don't know. We have all heard that before but it is particularly true when it comes to The Blessing of Abraham and The Curse of The law.

Mary and I were attending a conference at Faith Life Church of Sarasota, Florida, which was being conducted by Pastor Keith Moore. When he came out we could just see The Blessing of God on him. A few minutes later he introduced Kenneth and Gloria Copeland and they stood up and acknowledged everyone.

We could absolutely see The Blessing of God on these two people. I leaned over to Mary and said, "I'll bet we are the only two people in this church tonight with the revelation that The Same Blessing that is on Brother Keith and Phyllis and Kenneth and Gloria Copeland is available to us."

A huge revelation to me was the fact that God did not pick out Keith and Phyllis Moore and Kenneth and Gloria Copeland to bestow The Blessing of Abraham upon, although they defiantly do have it. The same Blessing that they have is available to me, or to any believer, if we will just increase our faith for it.

Most people do not know that God actually wants them to live a Blessed life. The **Same** Blessing that has been passed down from Abraham to all of his seed is actually available to them, belongs to them, and is their inheritance. If they **had this revelation,** they would be after The Blessing of Abraham like Jacob went after The Blessing. He held on to God all night long, until The Lord Blessed him.

If you ask almost any born again believer how they are doing, they will tell you that they are blessed. Many of them will even say that they are blessed and highly favored. They believe they are blessed, when the truth of the matter is they are experiencing little blessings here and there. Some have even had good size blessings and some have even experienced major blessings, but they are not walking in The Fullness of The Blessing of Abraham.

I have even heard people, who are sick and can't pay their bills, talking about how Blessed they are. Sadly, they do not even know what The Blessing is.

People mistake a blessing for THE Blessing and there is a <u>huge difference.</u>

If you ask people, in any church, what they need, they will tell you it is financial, or in many cases, healing.

Many of God's people are having major problems with their health, including high blood pressure, diabetes, arthritis, heart disease, headaches and so on. This should not be, because The Blessing of Abraham brings healing.

The Blessing of Abraham is all of the Blessings combined and The Curse of The Law is all of the curses combined.

Other people are struggling to pay their bills and working two, or sometimes even three jobs, to make ends meet. They are trying to believe God to come up with enough money to make their rent and car payments. This also should not be, because the Blessing of Abraham brings abundance.

It is just as easy to develop your faith for The Blessing of Abraham as it is to develop your faith for money to pay the rent.

It is not now and it never will be, God's intention for any of His people to be sick, or broke. Our Heavenly Father is a good God. He is wonderful, He loves us and He only wants the very best for us, at all times.

Without the Blessing of Abraham, people are limited to what they can do for themselves.

The <u>same exact Blessing</u> that was on Abraham belongs to us. Not <u>a</u> blessing, or <u>a little</u> blessing but <u>The Fullness</u> of The Blessing.

The Blessing of Abraham is our inheritance. It is available to all of God's people **and it will cause you to live your life on a level that you never imagined.** It will also bring into your life, health and abundance, to the extent that your family and friends will want to know what has happened in your life. You will be able to tell them how they can have the same thing.

God **needs** you to live in the Fullness of The Blessing of Abraham. It is the goodness of God that draws people to repentance. When people see the goodness of God manifested in your life, they will want what you have. People will listen when you tell them about Jesus and will even go to church with you.

Make a Major Decision right now that you are going to have the Fullness of The Blessing of Abraham in your life.

By the time you finish reading this book, your thinking will have changed, and your mind will have been renewed. You will be on your way to living the **Blessed Life of Abundance** that God intended for you since the foundation of the world.

I can guarantee you three things:

1. This book will change your life forever.

2. You will read this book over and over.

3. You will tell all of your friends and your family, about this book.

Sometimes, as I was writing this book, God would give me revelation of His Word that would take my breath away. I would have to stop and just worship The Lord and thank Him for His goodness.

You are going to see some statements in this book that no one has ever taught before, that I know of. Check the Scriptures regarding every statement for yourself.

Say this out loud, "God does not want me to be sick, God does not want me to be broke. God wants me to live in the Blessing of Abraham because the Blessing of Abraham is my inheritance."

Say out loud, "<u>I am absolutely going to live the rest of my life with The fullness of The Blessing of Abraham in my life.</u>"

Be a Blessing to others and help to spread this message, of The Blessing, to the entire body of Christ.

Send everyone you know <u>a link</u> to where they can get a copy of this book for themselves.

Chapter 1

NOTHING ELSE MATTERS
BUT THE BLESSING

To Be Blessed is to be Spiritually Programmed for Success in <u>Every Area</u> of your life.

Genesis 1:26-28 And God said, Let us make man in our image, after our likeness: and let them have dominion over the fish of the sea, and over the fowl of the air, and over the cattle, and over all the earth, and over every creeping thing that creeps upon the earth.

1

²⁷ So God created man in his own image, in the image of God created he them; male and female created he them.

²⁸ And God blessed them, and God said unto them, Be fruitful, and multiply, and replenish the earth, and subdue it: and have dominion over the fish of the sea, and over the fowl of the air, and over every living thing that moves upon the earth.

Genesis 2:7-8 And the LORD God formed man of the dust of the ground, and breathed into his nostrils the breath of life; and man became a living soul. 8 And the Lord God planted a garden eastward in Eden; and there he put the man whom he had formed.

God created man and his wife and put them in the Garden of Eden. He empowered them to be fruitful and to multiply and to replenish the earth. I believe Brother Copeland is absolutely right when he said, that God intended for the entire earth to be the Garden of Eden.

The Blessing, and people living in The Garden of Eden, was God's original plan for all of mankind and that has not and will never change.

God had us in mind for The Blessing from the foundation of the world.

I also believe that the Garden of Eden was exactly the same as what we will find in Heaven, when we get there. We will see a beautiful Garden, with trees full of delicious fruit, where everything is provided in abundance for God's people.

There was no sickness in The Garden of Eden, so we know that healing is a part of The Blessing for God's Covenant people.

There was no poverty in the Garden of Eden, so we know that Prosperity is a part of The Blessing for God's Covenant people.

> **Deuteronomy 11:21 That your days may be multiplied and the days of your children, in the land which the LORD swore unto your fathers to give them, as the <u>days of Heaven</u> upon the earth.**

God intended for life in the Promised Land to be like days of Heaven.

Sickness and poverty are subject to change and The Blessing is the changer.

When God Blessed Abraham, He planned for us to inherit that exact same Blessing.

WHEN IT COMES TO <u>SUCCESS OR FAILURE,</u> NOTHING ELSE MATTERS BUT THE BLESSING OF ABRAHAM.

If you have received the Blessing of Abraham, success will come easy. If you have not received The Blessing, you will struggle for success and it does not matter how gifted you are, how smart you are, how well educated, or talented or even how anointed you are.

(I'll bet that explains a lot of things, doesn't it?)

The Anointing of God and The Blessing of God are two different things.

A person can be highly Anointed for ministry and called of God, but if they have not received The Blessing of Abraham, they will struggle for success.

A person can be Blessed of God with little or no Anointing on their lives, yet still be very successful in ministry. This explains why Ministers, who seem to have little or no anointing, and do not even teach the Word of Faith, can have very successful churches.

The Blessing of Abraham is a huge factor in business

A person who has received The Blessing will be successful in whatever type of business or work they do. It does not matter how little education or training they have, or even how they go about conducting their business.

I knew a man who owned a large automobile dealership, who absolutely made all of the wrong moves. Every time things were going good, he would make major changes, which would cause huge problems. I should know I worked for him. Every dumb move he made seemed to work out in the end, no matter how many problems it caused and how much the people who worked for him suffered. In the end, he retired as a multimillionaire, because **nothing else matters but The Blessing.**

If you are struggling to be successful, The Blessing of Abraham will cause success to come easy.

I have known other smart, well educated professional people who started businesses, which were well funded. They made all the right moves, hired all the right people, had all the right connections and went broke.

The difference is The Blessing.

When you combine The Blessing of Abraham with smart business people you get John D. Rockefeller, The man who owns Chick-fil-A, the owner of Hobby Lobby and almost all of the Jewish business people.

Have you ever wondered why some Christian musicians and singers, with what seems to be incredible talent, are not successful in drawing an audience to their music? While at the same time singers, with obviously much less ability, are hugely successful? The difference is The Blessing.

You cannot have the Blessing of Abraham and be poor at the same time.

You do not even need to be smart, well educated, or good looking (like me) to be highly successful, if you have received The Blessing of the Lord.

<u>Nothing else matters</u> but The Blessing of God, When it comes to being successful.

Proverbs 10:22. The Blessing of the LORD, it makes rich, and He adds no hard work or toil with it. The Blessing of The Lord brings <u>easy success</u> to everyone who receives it.

The Blessing of The Lord does indeed bring riches, but it also makes every area of your life much better.

The Blessing is an empowerment, imparted on a person, so that they may become successful in every area of their life.

Churches should make it a top priority to get people Blessed with The Blessing of Abraham. The Blessing on the lives of people will bring healing, prosperity, success and empower every area of their life.

People who have received The Blessing do not work to earn a living; they work to be a Blessing and because they want to.

THE BLESSING OF ABRAHAM ON ABRAHAM

Genesis 12:1-3. Now the LORD had said unto Abram, Get thee out of thy country, and from thy kindred, and from thy father's house, unto a land that I will show thee:

²And I will make of thee a great nation, and I will bless thee, and make thy name great; and thou shall be a blessing:

³And I will bless them that bless thee, and curse him that curses thee: and in thee shall all families of the earth be blessed.

Galatians 3:8. And the scripture, foreseeing that God would justify the heathen through faith, preached before the gospel unto Abraham, saying, In thee shall all nations be blessed.

The Gospel that God preached to Abraham was that the Blessing was going to come through him. By this scripture alone, we know that The Blessing is a huge part of the Gospel.

Abraham's Blessing was conditional upon his obedience to leave his family and his country and go wherever God wanted him to go. Sometimes, receiving The Blessing of Abraham is conditional, if God has something He wants you to do. I tell God every day, Lord, show me what I need to know and tell me what I need to do.

There are seven parts to The Blessing that God spoke over Abraham.

1. The Promised Land. This was meant to be a Garden of Eden for Israel.

2. You will start a great nation of people. Multiply.

3. You are empowered for success in every area of your life.

4. Your name will be well known. This happens to everyone who gets the Blessing.

5. You will be a Blessing. The more you are Blessed, the more of a Blessing you can be to others.

6. I will Bless people who Bless you and curse people who curse you. The same thing applies to you because people who Bless you will be Blessed.

7. The Blessing will come to all people through you. That is why it is called The Blessing of Abraham. This will happen to us on a smaller scale. Other people will receive the Blessing because they will want what we have.

We have a Garden of Eden Covenant with God.

Isaiah 51:3 For the LORD shall comfort Zion: he will comfort all her waste places; and he will make her wilderness like Eden, and her desert like the garden of the LORD; joy and gladness shall be found therein, thanksgiving, and the voice of melody.

The Blessing brought Garden of Eden like conditions into the life of Abraham, Isaac, Jacob and Joseph and that is what it does in the life of everyone who receives it and it does not take circumstances or situations into consideration.

Material Abundance is a huge part of The Blessing

Genesis 13:1-13 And Abram went up out of Egypt, he, and his wife, and all that he had, and Lot with him, into the south.

² And Abram was very rich in cattle, in silver, and in gold.

A Blessed person is empowered to succeed.

⁵ And Lot also, which went with Abram, had flocks, and herds, and tents.

⁶ And the land was not able to bear them, that they might dwell together: for their substance was great, so that they could not dwell together.

⁷ And there was a strife between the herdsmen of Abram's cattle and the herdsmen of Lot's cattle: and the Canaanite and the Perizzite dwelled then in the land.

⁸ And Abram said unto Lot, Let there be no strife, I pray thee, between me and thee, and between my herdsmen and thy herdsmen; for we be brethren.

⁹ Is not the whole land before thee? separate thyself, I pray thee, from me: if thou wilt take the left hand, then I will go to the right; or if thou depart to the right hand, then I will go to the left.

¹⁰ And Lot lifted up his eyes, and beheld all the plain of Jordan, that it was well watered everywhere, before the LORD destroyed Sodom and Gomorrah, even as the garden of the LORD, like the land of Egypt, as thou comes unto Zoar.

¹¹ Then Lot chose him all the plain of Jordan; and Lot journeyed east: and they separated themselves the one from the other.

¹² Abram dwelled in the land of Canaan, and Lot dwelled in the cities of the plain, and pitched his tent toward Sodom.

¹³ But the men of Sodom were wicked and sinners before the LORD exceedingly.

This passage of scripture is very important because it shows what happened to Abraham after God said He would Bless him. He had favor when he went into Egypt and in very short order, he became VERY RICH.

The Blessing of Abraham will give you things you never imagined.

Lot also became rich because of his association with his Uncle Abraham. However, even though Lot chose the best of the land when they split up, he lost everything he had. He was no longer under the influence of The Blessed man. Lot should have sold some of his herds and stayed with his Uncle.

Even living on the best land could not prosper Lot, because he went there without The Blessing. Abraham increased and became more prosperous while living on the land that was not as good. The Blessing was on him and **<u>nothing else matters but The Blessing.</u>**

Genesis 14:10-17 And the vale of Siddim was full of slimepits; and the kings of Sodom

and Gomorrah fled, and fell there; and they that remained fled to the mountain.

[11] And they took all the goods of Sodom and Gomorrah, and all their victuals, and went their way.

[12] And they took Lot, Abram's brother's son, who dwelt in Sodom, and his goods, and departed.

[13] And there came one that had escaped, and told Abram the Hebrew; for he dwelt in the plain of Mamre the Amorite, brother of Eshcol, and brother of Aner: and these were confederate with Abram.

[14] And when Abram heard that his brother was taken captive, he armed his trained servants, born in his own house, three hundred and eighteen, and pursued them unto Dan.

[15] And he divided himself against them, he and his servants, by night, and smote them,

and pursued them unto Hobah, which is on the left hand of Damascus.

¹⁶ And he brought back all the goods, and also brought again his Nephew Lot, and his goods, and the women also, and the people.

¹⁷ And the king of Sodom went out to meet him after his return from the <u>slaughter </u>of Chedorlaomer, and of the kings that were with him, at the valley of Shaveh, which is the king's dale.

Lot, who was now living down in the plain, was taken captive with all of his family and goods. Abraham recovered everything that had been stolen. He did it with 318 of his servants who he armed, against 4 kings and their armies who were trained for war and heavily armed. Abraham and his servants slaughtered them, because **<u>nothing else matters but The Blessing.</u>**

When you have received The Blessing of Abraham, you are able to do things you could not do before.

Genesis 21:1-2 And the LORD visited Sarah as he had said, and the LORD did unto Sarah as he had spoken.

² For Sarah conceived, and bare Abraham a son in his old age, at the set time of which God had spoken to him.

Abraham and Sarah had a baby boy when he was 100 years old and she was 90. They had developed their faith in The Blessing that God had promised. Their age was no longer an issue, because **nothing else matters but The Blessing.**

THE BLESSING OF ABRAHAM ON ISAAC

Genesis 26 And there was a famine in the land, beside the first famine that was in the days of Abraham. And Isaac went unto Abimelech, king of the Philistines unto Gerar.

² And the LORD appeared unto him, and said, Go not down into Egypt; dwell in the land which I shall tell thee of:

³ Sojourn in this land, and I will be with thee, and will bless thee; for unto thee, and unto thy seed, I will give all these countries, and <u>I will perform the</u> oath which I swore unto Abraham your father;

When you have received the Fullness of the Blessing, God will perform the same oath in your life that he swore to Abraham.

⁴ And I will make thy seed to multiply as the stars of heaven, and will give unto thy seed all these countries; and in thy seed shall all the nations of the earth be blessed;

⁵ Because that Abraham obeyed my voice, and kept my charge, my commandments, my statutes, and my laws.

⁶ And Isaac dwelt in Gerar:

¹² Then Isaac sowed in that land, and received in the same year an hundredfold: and the LORD blessed him.

¹³ **And the man waxed great, and went forward, and grew until he became very great:**

¹⁴ **For he had possession of flocks, and possession of herds, and great store of servants: and the Philistines envied him.**

The famine was part of the Curse, but
The Blessing of Abraham overcame the Famine in the
life of Isaac.

After his father, Abraham, had died, Isaac had to develop his own faith for the Blessing. Isaac was not able to feed his family because there was a famine in the land. God told him not to go down into Egypt to find food. Stay in the land that He would show him, and He would Bless him. Once again, the Blessing was conditional.

Notice that God did not tell Isaac that He would provide for him if he stayed. I am quite sure he would have been very happy just to have enough food to feed his family at this point. No, God said to stay there and He would Bless Him. There is a HUGE DIFFERENCE between being provided for and being Blessed.

Isaac stayed as God had instructed him to and sowed DURING A FAMINE and reaped 100%. Who in their right mind would plant seeds during a famine? Only a person who had The Blessing of Abraham upon them that's who and then **it doesn't matter** if it rains or not.

The Blessing of Abraham does not take any situations, circumstances, or bad economies into consideration. It just creates the Garden of Eden in the life of anyone who receives it and it will do the same thing in your life.

Isaac became very rich with flocks and herds and servants. So rich in fact, that the Philistines became afraid of him. He increased greatly DURING A FAMINE, because **nothing else matters but The Blessing**.

THE BLESSING OF ABRAHAM ON JACOB

After Jacob and his Mother had deceived everyone and had the Blessing of Abraham spoken over him by his father Isaac, he was sent to his uncle's house to stay until his brother cooled off and to find a wife. When he set out on his journey he took nothing with him except a peanut butter sandwich, a walking stick and The Blessing. I may be wrong about the peanut butter sandwich, but I do know for sure that he had The Blessing of Abraham upon him.

While he was there his Uncle deceived him, lowered his wages 10 times and was greatly Blessed himself, because he had a Blessed person working for him. If you own a business, try to hire Blessed people.

Genesis 30:25-31 And it came to pass, when Rachel had born Joseph, that Jacob said unto Laban, Send me away, that I may go unto mine own place, and to my country.

26 Give me my wives and my children, for whom I have served thee, and let me go: for thou know my service which I have done thee.

27 And Laban said unto him, I pray thee, if I have found favor in your eyes, stay here: for I have learned by experience that the LORD hath blessed me for thy sake.

28 And he said, Appoint me thy wages, and I will give it.

²⁹ And he said unto him, Thou know how I have served thee, and how thy cattle was with me.

³⁰ For it was little which thou had before I came, and it is now increased unto a multitude; and the LORD hath blessed thee since my coming: and now when shall I provide for mine own house also?

³¹ And he said, what shall I give thee? And Jacob said <u>thou shall not give me any thing</u>: if thou will do this thing for me, I will again feed and keep thy flock.

Finally, Jacob told his Uncle to stop paying him wages for keeping his cattle and flocks. Instead of wages, he would keep the speckled and spotted animals for his pay. Now he was totally depended on God and the Blessing of Abraham to provide for him. In just a few years he became very rich, because **<u>nothing else matters but The Blessing.</u>**

THE BLESSING OF ABRAHAM ON JOSEPH.

Genesis 37:3-11 Now Israel loved Joseph more than all his children, because he was

the son of his old age: and he made him a coat of many colors.

⁴ And when his brethren saw that their father loved him more than all his brethren, they hated him, and could not speak peaceably unto him.

⁵ And Joseph dreamed a dream, and he told it to his brethren: and they hated him yet the more.

⁶ And he said unto them, Hear, I pray you, this dream which I have dreamed:

⁷ For, behold, we were binding sheaves in the field, and, lo, my sheaf arose, and also stood upright; and, behold, your sheaves stood round about, and made obeisance to my sheaf.

⁸ And his brethren said to him, Shall thou indeed reign over us? or shall thou indeed have dominion over us? And they hated him yet the more for his dreams, and for his words.

⁹ And he dreamed yet another dream, and told it his brethren, and said, Behold, I

have dreamed a dream more; and, behold, the sun and the moon and the eleven stars made obeisance to me.

¹⁰ And he told it to his father, and to his brethren: and his father rebuked him, and said unto him, What is this dream that thou hast dreamed? Shall I and thy mother and thy brethren indeed come to bow down ourselves to thee to the earth?

¹¹ And his brethren envied him; but his father observed the saying.

Joseph's brothers did not like him in the first place. He would keep their father informed whenever his brothers weren't doing what they were suppose to do. When he told them of his dream, in which they would all bow down to him, they decided to kill him. However, instead of killing him, they sold him as a slave down into Egypt. Be careful who you tell your dreams to.

Genesis 39:1-5 And Joseph was brought down to Egypt; and Potiphar, an officer of Pharaoh, captain of the guard, an Egyptian,

bought him of the hands of the Ishmeelites, which had brought him down thither.

² And the LORD was with Joseph, and he was a prosperous man; and he was in the house of his master the Egyptian.

³ And his master saw that the LORD was with him, and that the LORD made all that he did to prosper in his hand.

⁴ And Joseph found grace in his sight, and he served him: and he made him overseer over his house, and all that he had he put into his hand.

⁵ And it came to pass from the time that he had made him overseer in his house, and over all that he had, that the LORD blessed the Egyptian's house for Joseph's sake; and the blessing of the LORD was upon all that he had in the house, and in the field.

Potiphar's wife tried to get Joseph to sleep with her. When he refused to "Sin against God," she claimed he attacked her and he was thrown into prison.

Genesis 39:20-23 And Joseph's master took him, and put him into the prison, a place where the king's prisoners were bound: and he was there in the prison.

²¹ But the LORD was with Joseph, and showed him mercy, and gave him favor in the sight of the keeper of the prison.

²² And the keeper of the prison committed to Joseph's hand all the prisoners that were in the prison; and whatsoever they did there, he was the doer of it.

²³ The keeper of the prison looked not to anything that was under his hand; because the LORD was with him, and that which he did, the LORD made it to prosper.

Joseph went into the prison with the Blessing of Abraham upon him. He had favor in that place and The Lord caused everything he did to prosper. Even if a person is in prison, **nothing else matters but The Blessing**.

The Blessing of Abraham overcomes all obstacles and circumstances in your life.

Two years later Joseph interpreted a dream for Pharaoh and became Prime Minister of Egypt. He woke up one morning in prison and went to bed that night in the palace. The Blessing can also turn your life around just that fast.

> **Genesis 41:39-41 And Pharaoh said unto Joseph, Forasmuch as God hath showed thee all this, there is none so discreet and wise as thou art:**
>
> **⁴⁰ Thou shall be over my house, and according unto thy word shall all my people be ruled: only in the throne will I be greater than thou.**
>
> **⁴¹ And Pharaoh said unto Joseph, See, I have set thee over all the land of Egypt.**

Under the guidance of Joseph, Egypt became a Garden of Eden, during a famine, because **nothing else matters but The Blessing**.

The entire country of Egypt was Blessed, because Joseph brought The Blessing of Abraham with him when he was sold into slavery. You should take The Blessing with you, everywhere you go, especially when you go to work.

The Blessing of Abraham opens doors that would otherwise be closed to you.

THE BLESSING OF ABRAHAM ON JOB

Job 1:1-3 There was a man in the land of Uz, whose name was Job; and that man was perfect and upright, and one that feared God, and eschewed evil.

² And there were born unto him seven sons and three daughters.

³ His substance also was seven thousand sheep, and three thousand camels, and five hundred yoke of oxen, and five hundred she asses, and a very great household; so that this man was the greatest of all the men of the east.

Job definitely had The Blessing of Abraham upon him. His **words of fear** brought the Blessing Wall down.

The devil came into his life, with the Curse of The Law, and he lost all that he had. If you feel fear, keep your mouth shut.

Job never cursed God but he did repent. I believe he repented of his words of fear, doubt and unbelief. God Blessed him again. The Blessing Wall went back up, and he increased until he had twice as much as he had before, because **nothing else matters but The Blessing.**

THE BLESSING OF ABRAHAM ON DAVID

1 Samuel 17:26 And David spoke to the men that stood by him, saying, What shall be done to the man that kills this Philistine, and takes away the reproach from Israel? for who is this uncircumcised Philistine, that he should defy the armies of the living God?

David is asking, who is this non-covenant person who is defying the armies of the Living God. David understood the covenant that Israel has with God. He is wondering why someone in their right mind, no matter how big they are, would dare to come against God's people. Sometimes, I wonder the same thing.

1 Samuel 17:38-40 And Saul armed David with his armor, and he put a helmet of brass upon his head; also he armed him with a coat of mail.

³⁹ And David girded his sword upon his armor, and he assayed to go; for he had not proved it. And David said unto Saul, I cannot go with these; for I have not proved them. And David put them off him.

⁴⁰ And he took his staff in his hand, and chose him five smooth stones out of the brook, and put them in a shepherd's bag which he had, even in a scrip; and his sling was in his hand: and he drew near to the Philistine.

David did not need the armor of Saul. He had The Blessing of Abraham on him. That was all he needed to kill the giant, **because nothing else matters but The Blessing.**

ALL OF GOD'S PROMISES ARE IN THE BLESSING.

Psalm 23 The LORD is my shepherd; I shall not want.

² He makes me to lie down in green pastures: he leads me beside the still waters.

³ He restores my soul: he leads me in the paths of righteousness for his name's sake.

⁴ Yea, though I walk through the valley of the shadow of death, I will fear no evil: for thou art with me; thy rod and thy staff they comfort me.

⁵ Thou preparers a table before me in the presence of mine enemies: thou anoints my head with oil; my cup runs over.

⁶ Surely goodness and mercy shall follow me all the days of my life: and I will dwell in the house of the LORD forever.

I know we ministers read this Psalm at funerals. However, this is actually the confession of a man who knows that he has the Blessing of Abraham. This should also be our confession.

It would also be a good idea to read about David's son, Soloman, the richest man who ever lived. He had The Blessing of Abraham upon him.

THE BLESSING OF ABRAHAM ON JESUS

Galatians 3:16 Now to Abraham and his seed were the promises made. He saith not, And to seeds, as of many; but as of one, And to thy seed, which is Christ.

Jesus came to the earth to redeem God's people and to bring back The Same Blessing that God had spoken over Adam and Eve. He was successful and now all we need to do is receive it by faith. You cannot separate Jesus from The Blessing of Abraham because it is what He came to restore, which gives us both life and abundance.

God needs for you to receive The Blessing because you are an ambassador for Christ and a reflection of God.

THE BLESSING IS BECAUSE OF ABRAHAM

God Blessed Isaac, because of Abraham.

God Blessed Jacob, because of Abraham.

God Blessed Joseph, because of Abraham.

God brought the people out of Egypt, because of Abraham.

God gives us power to get wealth, because of Abraham.

Jesus healed the woman in the Temple, because of Abraham.

God has Blessed me, because of Abraham.

The Blessing belongs to all born again people, because Jesus restored unto us, The Blessing of Abraham. You have a right to be Blessed.

Maybe you should not receive The Blessing

If you do not want to have wealth and riches in your house, do not receive The Blessing. Psalms 112:3

If you do not want to succeed in everything that you do, do not receive The Blessing. Psalms 1:3

If you do not want to be satisfied during a famine, or a bad economy, do not receive The Blessing. Psalms 37:19

If you do not want to be rich, do not receive The Blessing. Proverbs 10:22

If you do not want you and your children to increase more and more, do not receive The Blessing. Psalms 115:13

If you do not want to live the abundant life Jesus came to provide for us, do not receive The Blessing. John 10:10

If you do not want peace in your life that unbelievers cannot understand, do not receive The Blessing. Philippians 4:7

If you do not want God to perform the same oath in your life that He performed in the life of Isaac, do not receive The Blessing. Genesis 26:3

If you do not want God to rebuke the devourer for your sake, do not receive The Blessing. Malachi 3:11

If you do not want to be Blessed like Jabez, do not receive The Blessing. 1 Chronicles 4:9-10

If you do not want people to know who you are, do not receive the Blessing. Genesis 12:2

If you do not want God to open the windows of Heaven and pour you out a Blessing that there is not enough room to receive it, do not receive The Blessing. Malachi 3:10

If you do not want to be surrounded by favor, do not receive the Blessing. Psalms 5:12

If you do not want your storehouse (bank account) to be full, do not receive the Blessing. Deuteronomy 28:8

If you do not want God to run your cup over, do not receive the Blessing. Psalms 23:5

If you do not want to live your life without wanting things, do not receive the Blessing. Psalms 34:8-10

If you do not want the Lord to take pleasure in your prosperity, do not receive the Blessing. Psalms 35:27

If you do not want to have lots of nice stuff, do not receive the Blessing. Deuteronomy 28:11

If you do not want God to give you the desires of your heart, do not receive the Blessing. Psalms 37:4

If you do not want a wall of Blessing around you, do not receive The Blessing. Job 1:10

If you do not want everything that you need given to you, do not receive The Blessing. Matthew 6:33

If you do not want the power to get wealth, do not receive The Blessing. Deut. 8:18

If you do not want to live a long life and have days of Heaven while you are on the earth, do not receive The Blessing. Deut 11:21

If you do not want houses you did not build, filled with nice things you did not buy, do not receive The Blessing. Deut. 6:10-11

If you do not want to leave an inheritance to your grandchildren, do not receive The Blessing. Proverbs 13:22

If you do not want to be a Blessing to others, do not receive the Blessing. Genesis 12:2

If you do not want God to supply all of your needs, according to His riches in Glory, do not receive The Blessing. Philippians 4:19

The reason God has Blessed us is so that His Kingdom and The Garden of Eden will be expanded and His Name will be Glorified.

Say out loud, "I have The Same Blessing that God spoke over Abraham, Isaac, Jacob and Joseph and it will quickly create the Garden of Eden in my life just like it did in their life."

Say out loud, "Father God, I know The Blessing of Abraham belongs to me. It is my birthright, and I receive it right now, in Jesus Name."

Be a Blessing to others and help spread the Word of God about The Blessing.

If you know anyone who should be living in The Blessing of Abraham, share this book with them.

Keep a copy of this book with you at all times so that you can sow it into the life of someone who really needs it.

Carry a copy of this book with you, when you go to church, and show it to everyone.

Chapter 2

THE CURSE OF THE LAW
AND REDEMPTION

If The Curse of The Law was not operating in your life, you would live in perfect health and become rich very quickly.

As you read this chapter, please understand that this is not from me. Most of it is not even from other people, although some of it is. The Lord literally took me through these revelations step by step. You will see how it all matches up with God's Word.

Galatians 3:13-14 Christ has redeemed us from the curse of the law, being made a curse for us for it is written, cursed is everyone who hangs on a tree, 14 so that The Blessing of Abraham can come on the Gentiles through Jesus Christ; that we might receive the promise that The Spirit made to Abraham, through faith.

These two verses tell us that Jesus redeemed us from the curse of the law so that we can have The Blessing of Abraham. If that is true, which it most certainly is, then why are so many Christians sick and broke? The answer is because most of God's people, even though they are redeemed, still have The Curse of The Law operating in their lives and this should not be.

Read on, you are about to get the curse of the law out of your life once and for all.

BECAUSE

The Curse of The Law must be removed from your life before you can Live in the Blessing of Abraham.

It is like trying to fill a glass full of water, with air, which is impossible. But, if you pour the water out, air will automatically come in and fill the glass. When you get rid of the curse of the law, The Blessing will automatically come in and fill your life. Then it is just a matter of developing your faith to live in The Blessing.

John 10:10 The thief cometh not, but for to steal, and to kill, and to destroy: I am come that they might have life, and that they might have it more abundantly.

This verse completely describes what the devil is all about and what Jesus came to the earth, to accomplish. The devil brings The Curse of The Law, which is all about stealing, killing and destroying. Jesus brings The Blessing, which is all about the abundant life. The abundant life, which Jesus is talking about here, only comes through The Blessing of Abraham. Before that can happen, the "thief" and his Curse of The Law must be evicted from your life.

The Curse of The Law came into the world, through the sin of Adam and will stay in your life, until it is commanded to leave in the Name of Jesus. It lost its legal right to be in our lives, when Jesus redeemed us, but it still must be evicted.

People spend so much of their time fighting small battles when getting rid of the entire Curse of the Law would solve all of their problems at one time and put them on the pathway to good health and prosperity.

<u>Please do not be deceived by how simple this really is.</u>

You can have The Blessing of Abraham operating in your life in one area and the Curse of The Law operating in another area. For example, many believers are prosperous, yet they are sick. Others are healthy, yet they are poor.

The devil cannot just pick out people to attack

You cannot imagine how many calls I get where people say, "Oh Pastor Jim I am under attack. Please do something, pray for me." I stop the attack by commanding the devil to leave them, in the Name of Jesus. Then I tell them that if they will just **keep their mouth shut** it will not happen again. Please understand that the devil has no access to your life <u>without your permission</u>.

WATCH YOUR WORDS!

We are going to remove the entire Curse of The Law from your life.

The first step in removing the curse of The Law is understanding redemption and to find out what we are redeemed from. Let's look at the Curse of The Law to see if we can find anything in there that **is going on in your life.**

Be sure to read Deuteronomy 28:15-68 which is the Curse of The Law.

To put it very simply, if you have _any_ disease, such as heart disease, cancer, arthritis, high blood pressure, diabetes, headaches, sickness, or illness _of any kind_, the Curse of the Law is working in your life.

If you have any poverty, lack, shortage of money, failure, having things you worked for taken from you, losing your stuff, having your things stolen from you. If you are not prospering in your ways, living a hard life, if your net worth has been decreasing; the Curse of The Law is operating in your life.

41

You must learn to recognize when The Curse of The Law is in your life, and if you admit that this is what is going on, you are on your way to living in the Blessing of Abraham.

This is what Jesus redeemed us from, but as you can plainly see, many people have this going on in their lives right now and this is going to stop.

I am here to tell you that the Curse of The Law was running wild in my life, but not anymore. I got rid of it and you can do the same thing.

Please understand that God is not cursing these people in Deuteronomy 28:15-68; He is allowing it to happen, by removing The Blessing.

The Blessing of Abraham and The Curse of the Law replace each other. When one goes out, the other comes in.

Either The Blessing of Abraham, or the Curse of The Law is operating in the life of everyone.

The Curse of The Law is punishment for the sin of Adam, which was passed down to all of us. Jesus took the Punishment. Now we can receive the same

42

Blessing that was upon Adam, Noah, Abraham, Isaac, Jacob and Joseph.

When Jesus said, "it is finished," He was talking about <u>total redemption.</u>

Just knowing that you are Redeemed, does not remove the Curse of The law from your life, just like knowing about Jesus, will not save anyone.

The curse of the law is in the life of every believer who has not commanded it to leave in the Name of Jesus. To do this you must understand your authority and have faith in **The Name of Jesus.** You must also believe in your heart and <u>not doubt</u> that what you say will come to pass. Mark 11:23.

You can confess that you are redeemed from the Curse of The Law, claim redemption and even sing, "Let the redeemed of the Lord say so," until you can't talk anymore, and nothing will happen. You can claim The Blessing, confess The Blessing and tell everyone that you are Blessed, but nothing will happen as long as the devil is in your life with the curse of the law.

The devil will never leave your life on his own.

Until the devil is told to leave and take The Curse of The Law with him, in the Name of Jesus, **he is going nowhere**. Why should he leave your life if he doesn't have to? He enjoys tormenting you because that is what he does. The more miserable, sick and poor he can keep you, the better he likes it.

You can also confess that you are Rich by the poverty of Jesus and healed by the stripes of Jesus, everyday all day for years. You may get some healings and financial Blessings, but as long as the Curse of The Law is still there, you will not see much in the way of lasting results.

Complaining about your situation or circumstances does not help either.

Like Cousin Eddie, the bad house guest, who shows up unannounced? You remember saying to him, several years earlier, at a family reunion, "You should come and see us sometime." Well, sometime has arrived. He bangs on the door and when you open it, he says in a loud voice, "I am here to take you up on your invitation." He messes up your house, eats all of your food, changes the channels on your television set and stays and stays and stays. You can complain all you want to, but Eddie likes staying there, living off of you and tormenting you. He will not leave your home until you absolutely tell him to leave, or you will call the police and have him arrested. Then he will go.

After Cousin Eddie is gone, would you invite him back again for just a little visit? Not likely. After the devil and the curse of the law are gone, watch your words, or you will invite them back. The devil is always waiting for an invitation to come back into your life.

The devil and the curse of the law
must be Evicted from your life.

Just because Christ has redeemed you, does not mean that the devil and the Curse of The Law have been removed from your life. However, you do not have to go through a long drawn out eviction process, in a complex court system, to get rid of the curse. Just use The Name of Jesus, to effect an **immediate eviction**.

Christ has indeed redeemed us, but He did not remove the curse of The Law from our lives. We must do the evicting ourselves in the Name of Jesus. We have the authority. Say, "Devil and Curse of The Law, get out now, in the Name of Jesus."

Just knowing that you are redeemed will not remove The Curse of The Law from your life, because the devil only responds to commands made in the name of Jesus.

Romans 5:17 For if by one man's offence death reigned by one; much more they which receive abundance of grace and of the gift of righteousness shall reign in life by one, Jesus Christ.)

We are called to rule and reign in this life but in order to do this we must get rid of the Curse of The Law in our life.

THE PROMISED LAND

The giants, who were big, strong, hairy and ugly, had to be driven out of the Promised Land before the children of Israel could live there. God had intended for the Promised Land to be like Heaven on earth, a Garden of Eden. Before we can live in our Garden of Eden, which for us is the Blessing of Abraham, we also must drive out the giants, which are the devils who are oppressing us and causing the Curse of The Law to be in our lives.

These devils that are causing the Curse of The Law to operate in your life are also ugly and they are extremely afraid of you because you are armed with the Name of Jesus. You do not need to fight your way through to get to the Promised Land. Under our new and better Covenant, all you need to do is speak to the devils in The Name of **Jesus**, which is the name that is above all names. They must obey you and leave your life, taking The Curse of The Law with them. Can you say thank You Jesus?

Do not be deceived by how simple this is.

CURSE OF SPIRITUAL DEATH

Genesis 2:17 But of the tree of the knowledge of good and evil, thou shall not eat of it: for in the day that you eat it thou shall surely die.

John 3:16 For God so loved the world, that he gave his only begotten Son, that whosoever believeth in him should not perish, but have everlasting life.

2 Corinthians 5:21 For he hath made him to be sin for us, who knew no sin; that we might be made the righteousness of God in him.

Adam brought the curse of spiritual death, which is separation from God, into the world by his sin. Jesus redeemed us, from the sin of Adam and of our own sins, and reconciled us back to God by the shedding of His blood. He suffered this punishment so we can spend eternity in Heaven.

Only a person who has led a perfect life and who has never sinned can redeem us from sin. Jesus never sinned, never had a bad thought and never made a mistake while He was on this earth.

CURSE OF THE HARD LIFE

Genesis 3:17 And unto Adam he said, Because thou hast hearkened unto the voice of thy wife, and hast eaten of the tree, of which I commanded thee, saying, Thou shall not eat of it: cursed is the ground for thy sake; in sorrow shalt thou eat of it all the days of thy life;

¹⁸ Thorns also and thistles shall it bring forth to thee; and thou shall eat the herb of the field;

¹⁹ In the sweat of thy face shall thou eat bread, till thou return unto the ground; for out of it was thou taken: for dust thou art, and unto dust shall thou return.

God is telling Adam that because of sin, the ground is now cursed. God just removed The Blessing and The Curse came in. Adam's Blessed life has changed into a hard life and the thorns are a sign of it.

Deuteronomy 28:23 And thy heaven that is over thy head shall be brass, and the earth that is under thee shall be iron. This is symbolic of a hard life in The Curse of The Law.

Who do we know who wore a crown of thorns, on His Head, when He went to the cross?

Matthew 27:28-30 And they stripped him, and put on him a scarlet robe.

²⁹ And when they had platted a crown of thorns, they put it upon his head, and a reed in his right hand: and they bowed the knee before him, and mocked him, saying, Hail, King of the Jews!

³⁰ And they spit upon him, and took the reed, and smote him on the head.

Jesus redeemed us from the curse of a hard life by wearing a crown of thorns, on His head, so that we can have a good life. He suffered this punishment so that we can have a good life.

Only a person who lived a wonderful life can redeem us from a hard life. I would say Jesus qualifies for that because He came down here from Heaven.

THE CURSE OF SICKNESS AND DISEASE

Read through Deuteronomy chapter 28:15-68 and you will see that sickness and disease are a large part of the curse of the law.

Deuteronomy 28:61 Also every sickness, and every plague, which is not written in the book of this law, them will the LORD bring upon thee, until thou be destroyed.

Isaiah 53:4-5 Surely he hath borne our griefs, and carried our sorrows: yet we did esteem him stricken, smitten of God, and afflicted. But he was wounded for our transgressions; he was bruised for our iniquities: the chastisement of our peace was upon him; and with his stripes we are healed.

1 Peter 2:24 Who his own self bare our sins in his own body on the tree, that we, being dead to sins, should live unto righteousness: by whose stripes ye were healed.

Jesus redeemed us from sickness and disease by the stripes He took on His back before he was crucified.

Only a person who was never sick a day in His life, can redeem us from sickness. Jesus went from living in perfect health, to being sick to the point of death when he was beaten on his back with a whip, to within an inch of His life, for our sake. He suffered this punishment so we could be healed.

CURSE OF POVERTY

Deuteronomy 28:29 And thou shall grope at noonday, as the blind gropes in darkness, and thou shall not prosper in thy ways: and thou shall be only <u>oppressed</u> and spoiled evermore, and no man shall save thee.

Poverty, lack and failure are all through the curse of the law in Chapter 28 of Deuteronomy.

2 Corinthians 8:9 For ye know the grace of our Lord Jesus Christ, that, though he was rich, yet for your sakes he became poor, that ye through his poverty might be rich.

Jesus redeemed us from the curse of poverty, by becoming poor.

Only a person who was rich can redeem us from poverty. Jesus went from walking on streets of gold, to having everything taken away from Him and hanging naked on a cross, which is as poor as a person can get. He suffered this punishment so we could be prosperous.

If you allow yourself to be sick, or to be poor, or to be living a hard life, you are allowing the devil to put the same punishment on you that Jesus suffered. That is double jeopardy.

The Blessing of Abraham cannot operate in the life of a person while the curse of the law is operating. The curse of the law can and will stay and operate until it is commanded to leave in the name of Jesus. Then, The Blessing will come in and create The Garden of Eden.

In the Garden of Eden, God removed The Blessing and it was replaced by the curse.

In our lives when the curse is commanded to leave in the Name of Jesus it will always be replaced by The Blessing.

The Blessing and the Curse of The Law <u>replace each other</u>. Either one or the other is going to be operating in every area of your life.

I will not permit the Curse of the law to operate in any area of my life because I have authority over it in the Name of Jesus.

UNNECESSARY SUFFERING

Any sickness, poverty, or living a hard life is suffering and is absolutely unnecessary because Jesus suffered in order to redeem us from all of these.

Acts 10:38 How God anointed Jesus of Nazareth with the Holy Ghost and with power: who went about doing good, and healing all who were <u>oppressed</u> of the devil; for God was with him.

The way Jesus healed these people was to cast out the devils, which were causing oppression in all who were sick.

All oppression is caused by the devil.

The Curse of The Law is oppression.
Deuteronomy 28:29

Poverty and Sickness are oppression of the devil.

Everything in Deuteronomy 28:15-68 is oppression of the devil.

Mark 16:17 And these signs shall follow them that believe; <u>In my name shall they cast out devils</u>; they shall speak with new tongues.

Mark 11:23 For verily I say unto you, That whosoever shall say unto this <u>mountain</u>, Be thou removed, and be thou cast into the sea; and shall not doubt in his heart, but shall believe that those things which he said shall come to pass; he shall have whatsoever he said.

The Curse of the Law may very well be the <u>Mountain</u> in your life, which Jesus was talking about, in Mark 11:23

The word mountain means an <u>obstacle, or a hindrance.</u> The Curse of The Law is a **huge obstacle or hindrance** in the life of anyone who has it operating on a daily basis. Jesus said that, "If we tell it to leave and believe that what

55

we say will come to pass and not doubt in our heart we will have what we say."

Every obstacle or hindrance in your life, in all probabilities, is part of the curse of the law. Is poverty an obstacle or hindrance, or can we use the word mountain, in the lives of people? It sure is! Is sickness an obstacle, hindrance, or mountain in the life of anyone who is suffering with it? Yes, yes and yes!

The key to moving the obstacle out of your life is having faith that your words will cause something to happen.

God is not in the mountain building business, He does not put obstacles or hindrances in your life and He does not remove them from your life. You allow them to come in with your words and you remove them with **faith filled words**. We must develop faith, that when we speak, our words will effect change.

The devil must have your permission to put obstacles or hindrances into your life. **Be careful what you say**.

Asking God to remove the curse (mountain) will not bring results.

You, as a believer, have authority over the devils which are causing the Curse of the Law. Jesus said, "Them that believe." If you are one of them that believe, you do not have to put up with the <u>oppression</u> of the curse. You can be healed of sickness, you can be healed of poverty and you can be healed of the Curse of The law in the Name of Jesus.

How would Jesus deal with The Curse of The law?

He would <u>tell it to leave</u> and that would be <u>the end of it</u>. You can do the same thing by using the Name of Jesus.

John 14:12 Verily, verily, I say unto you, He that believeth on me, <u>the works that I do shall he do also</u>; and greater works than these shall he do; because I go unto my Father.

Gloria Copeland said that everything changed when they got a revelation that they had authority over the Curse of The Law in their lives. Everything changed for me when I got a revelation that the Curse of The Law, which was operating in my life, was being caused by the same devils that Jesus cast out when He healed all who were oppressed of the devil in Acts 10:38.

THE KEY TO RECEIVING THE BLESSING

I woke up one morning and I heard an audible voice inside my belly say, in an audible voice, "How God anointed Jesus of Nazareth with the Holy Ghost and with power who went about doing good and healing all who were oppressed of the devil." I jumped out of bed, ran and got my Bible and opened it to Acts 10:38. The Lord had been telling me, in an audible voice, in my spirit, for over two weeks, that the key to receiving The Blessing was in Mark Chapter 16. In verse 17, of that chapter, Jesus said, "In My Name they shall cast out devils." Now I knew the answer. I just needed to cast out the devils, which were causing The Curse of The Law, which is oppression, from my life.

GET A REVELATION OF MARK 16:17 AND ACTS 10:38

Then it was just a matter of me commanding the devil that was causing oppression of The Curse of The Law, to leave me in the Name of Jesus. That was the end of it and everything changed. Glory to God, you can do the same thing.

Kenneth and Gloria Copeland told the story of how, several years after they were saved, they received a revelation of redemption. He then stood up and rebuked the curse in the Name of Jesus. It immediately lost its authority over them and dried up. The Blessing then began to expand around them and grow. They were soon out of debt and began to increase. **That is how it works every time.** Listen to Brother Copeland's teachings on The Blessing in the archives of the Believers Voice of Victory Television Program.

The key to receiving the Blessing of Abraham is to remove the devil and the curse of the law from your life, in the Name of Jesus. When the curse of the law is gone the Blessing comes in. As your faith for The Blessing and in The Blessing increases, you will see it manifested more and more in your life. However, once the curse is gone, you will absolutely begin to see results very quickly.

The Curse of The Law will stay in your life until you, or someone commands it, and the devil who is causing it, to leave, in the Name of Jesus.

All sickness and disease is oppression, caused by the devil.

All poverty and lack is oppression, caused by the devil.

If it is caused by the devil, it can be cast out in The Name of Jesus

The Curse of The Law is **oppression,** caused by the devil, so you must cast it, and the devil who is causing the oppression, out in the Name of Jesus, or have someone do it for you and then you will be free of the curse. **How simple is this?**

You must know the authority of your words and have faith in The Name of Jesus to make it happen.

Philippians 2:10 That at the name of Jesus, every knee should bow, of things in Heaven, and things in earth, and things under the earth.

Matthew 16:19 And I will give unto thee the keys of the kingdom of Heaven: and <u>whatsoever thou shall bind on earth shall be bound in heaven</u>: and whatsoever thou shall loose on earth shall be loosed in heaven.

Say, "You devil who is causing the Curse of the Law, leave my life, right now. I bind you and shut you down in the Name of Jesus. Curse of the Law, you

leave my life right now. I bind you and shut you down in The Name of Jesus."

If you say that out loud and believe it and not doubt in your heart, that what you say shall come to pass, God will cause it to happen from Heaven. You will be free of The Curse of The Law. The Blessing of Abraham will begin to operate in your life. Things will soon begin to change for you.

THE NAME OF JESUS IS THE SHORTCUT TO THE BLESSING

You can come against all of the curses individually, as they cause problems, or just command the devil and The Entire Curse of The Law to leave at one time, in the Name of Jesus and be done with it.

You can also command the devil and the Curse of The Law to come out of the lives of people, in your family, if you are the person who has spiritual authority.

God will bind the devil, from operating The Curse of The Law in your life, from Heaven, if you bind him in the name of Jesus.

Casting out the Curse of the Law, in the Name of Jesus, will erect a **WALL OF REDEMPTION** between you and the devil who brings oppression and the curse.

NOW WATCH YOUR WORDS!

Proverbs 18:21 Your tongue has the power of life and death over you: and you shall live by the words that you speak.

Have you ever noticed that children of rich people will almost always be rich as adults and children of poor people will usually be poor as adults? These are Generational Blessings and Generational Curses.

GENERATIONAL CURSES

Many, many years ago, before I was saved, I used to smoke cigarettes. As I was lighting up, one fine day, I said to my father, "I am going to quit smoking." He looked at me and said, "You will smoke till the day you die." I replied, "No, I really am going to quit."

Well, I could not stop. Even after I got saved a few years later I would hide cigarettes so no one would know I was still smoking. I was working in a used car business and was telling everyone about Jesus. Hundreds of people got saved and healed. I was still smoking, not much but I just could not completely quit.

Finally, one day I was listening to an old Derek Prince tape on Blessings and Curses. The Lord showed me a vision of my Father, who was now dead, telling me that I would smoke until the day I died.

I stood up and said. "In the name of Jesus, I break that curse my father spoke over me about smoking and I declare that I will stop smoking." I then went back to my desk and lit up a cigarette. I really did not think much more about it but two weeks later I stopped smoking for good and have never had any more desire to smoke. That curse, which had been spoken over me, had been broken.

A generational curse cannot be overcome,
but it can be broken.

A generational curse can be started as easily as a man I once overheard, who said, "Every man in this family dies young of heart problems." I am quite sure he did not realize that he had just cursed every male off spring he would ever have. The curse of heart disease will run in his family until the curse he had spoken, is broken.

Breaking a generational curse in the Name of Jesus is like revoking the devil's invitation to come into your life and cause destruction. The devil cannot come in uninvited; he can only come in by invitation. You or one of your ancestors had to have extended this invitation to the devil, by speaking wrong words.

Examples of Generational curses:

A Father, who tells his son that he will never amount to anything, or says, "You will never be successful," has just cursed the entire offspring of his son, for generations to come.

Any sickness or disease that runs in the family is the result of a curse.

Heart disease is a terrible curse that runs in families.

Types of cancer that tend to run in families, such as breast cancer.

Also mental illness, lack of intelligence, alcoholism, domestic abuse and failure are often the result of generational curses.

Poverty is without a doubt a huge generational curse.

A financial curse could have been spoken in your family last week, or hundreds of years ago and still have a tremendous effect on your income.

Many of the curses mentioned in Deuteronomy Chapter 28 are generational curses and have been handed down.

These curses will run in families until they are broken, in The Name of Jesus.

If you notice anything that is not good going on in your life, which was also affecting the lives of people in your family who are older than you, you may be dealing with a generational curse.

Every curse is caused by a devil and if you bind it in the name of Jesus, it will be bound from Heaven. That curse will leave your life and will stay gone unless you curse yourself again with your words.

BREAK THE CURSE.

If poverty is in your life, just say, "I break the curse of poverty in my life and in my family in the name of Jesus. It is just that easy to break a curse if you have faith in your words. You can do the same thing with any curse that is running in your family and things will immediately begin to change.

NEVER USE THE WORD <u>DAMN</u> WHEN TALKING ABOUT YOURSELF, ANYONE UNDER YOUR AUTHORITY, OR ANYTHING THAT YOU OWN.

The word damn, means to curse, or to empower for failure, or destruction.

If you say something like, "That damn kid," when referring to your child, you have just cursed your child.

Other popular things to damn: That damn car. That damn dog. That damn house. I hate my damn job. Those damn people who work for me.

I WILL NEVER SAY MY DOG IS STUBBORN.

I was out walking my <u>wonderful</u> dog, Muffy, one day, and she decided that she did not want to walk. She sat down and would not move. One of my neighbors, who was standing close by said, "She sure is stubborn." I did not reply. I said, "Come on Muffy, let's go." She still would not move. My neighbor then said, "She is stubborn, come on, say it, say it, she is a stubborn dog." I looked at her and said, "Muffy is not stubborn, she is a good dog." If I had agreed with her, I would have owned a stubborn dog. Muffy has always been and will always be a great dog.

NOT ME!

I was out walking Muffy another fine evening in the community we lived in. Several neighbors were gathered on the street and were talking about a man who was dying of cancer in a hospice center. Someone said, "Well, I guess that is where we are all going to end up." People nodded their head in agreement but I said, "Not me." Everyone looked at me like I was from outer space. The same man said, "You must know something we don't know." I said,

"I do, that is not going to happen to me." If you agree when someone curses themselves, you get it to.

CHURCH CAN BE A DANGEROUS PLACE.

Mary and I were visiting a large church last year when, during the sermon, the Pastor said, "Trouble is going to come to you." We could hear people say Amen all over the sanctuary and I said in a rather loud voice. "Not to me it's not." People all around turned and looked at me. I said, "I am not going to agree with that." I said to Mary, "Everyone who agreed with that statement should duck, because they just gave the devil permission to bring trouble into their lives." Be careful when you say Amen, (so be it) even in church.

Be careful when agreeing with what people say.

NEVER SAY:

I keep getting sick.

I can't get over this.

Bad things always happen to me.

I must be losing my mind.

The very popular, it's just one thing after another.

I can't do this.

I can't afford this.

I will never get these bills paid.

People don't like me.

I never have enough money.

I can't lose weight.

I can't stop smoking, drinking, etc.

Never use the words, "**I can't**," when talking about yourself.

If you do say any of these things and believe what you say, you have just given the devil the legal right to come back. He will be loosed from Heaven and the Curse of

The Law will be back in your life until it is commanded to leave again in the Name of Jesus.

God allows things to happen because we allow it.

There is a connection between what we say here and what is bound or loosed from heaven.

All born again believers are redeemed. However, only those who receive redemption by faith, and take authority over the Curse of The Law, will live in The Blessing of Abraham. The rest will live under the Curse of the Law and this includes many good born again believers, who love The Lord with all their heart.

You do not have to live with The Curse of The law or have Generational Curses operating in your life.

Summary:

The Blessing of the Lord will make you rich and the Curse of The Law will make you poor. They are opposites.

To get healed you must first command the devil, which is causing the oppression, to come out and then believe you receive your healing by the stripes of Jesus.

The Curse of the Law and the Blessing of Abraham replace each other.

Just knowing you are redeemed does not remove the Curse of The Law from your life.

What the devil comes for in John 10:10, is stealing, killing and destroying, which is actually the curse of the law.

The abundant life Jesus is talking about in John 10:10, only comes through the Blessing of Abraham and that is what He came to restore for us.

All of The Blessings listed in Deuteronomy 28:1-14 are part of The Blessing of Abraham and belong to you, if you are a born again believer.

All of the curses found in Deuteronomy 28:15-68 are part of the curse of the law. If you can find anything in that passage of scripture, which is going on in your life, you are redeemed from it and should not have it.

Jesus provided total Redemption for us. It is finished.

Anything under The Curse of The Law is a curse. We have authority over it, in The Name of Jesus.

Spiritual death, which is separation from God, sickness, poverty and the hard life, was the punishment that God demanded for sin.

No one can be saved without a revelation that Christ redeemed us from sin.

By shedding His Blood and by His death on the cross, Jesus took the punishment and redeemed us from sin. 2 Corinthians 5:21

By His stripes Jesus took the punishment, and redeemed us from sickness, so that we can be healed. 1 Peter 2:24

By His poverty Jesus took the punishment, and redeemed us from poverty, so we can be rich. 2 Corinthians 8:9

By wearing a crown of thorns, Jesus redeemed us from the hard life, so we could have a good life. Genesis 3:17-19 Matthew 27:28-30

Jesus does not need you to help Him with redemption by your suffering. In other words, any suffering that you may go through is completely unnecessary.

Can you say thank you Jesus?

Say out loud, "In the Name of Jesus you devil, who has been causing the Curse of The Law to operate in my life, LEAVE ME NOW, IN THE NAME OF JESUS and take The Curse of The Law with you."

Say out loud, "I am absolutely 100% redeemed from the Curse of The Law by the Blood of Jesus, the stripes of Jesus, the poverty of Jesus and the crown of thorns that Jesus wore when He was crucified."

Say out loud, "I have authority over The Curse of the Law and I have commanded it to leave my life, in the Name of Jesus, and it is gone forever."

Tell everyone you know, who needs the Curse of The Law removed from their life, about this book, or send them a link where they can get their own book.

Join people around the world and listen to Pastor Jim's Free Sermons on The Blessing, Redemption and Increase at www.increasenow.com

Chapter 3

THE SPOKEN BLESSING

The Blessing of Abraham must be voice activated by someone in authority to do so.

You cannot activate The Blessing of Abraham in your own life, or the life of anyone else, unless you understand your authority to do so and have faith in your own words.

Genesis 1:26 And God said, Let us make man in Our image, after our likeness: and let them have dominion over the fish of the sea, and over the fowl of the air, and over the cattle, and over all the earth, and over every creeping thing that creeps upon the earth.

God created people in "Our image" which means that we have are **spirit body beings,** just like God. Our spirit lives in our earthly body made from dirt. The Spirit Body of God does not live in an earthly body. Now I'm sure you would like to see some scriptures for this, so here they are.

Exodus 33:18-23 And he said, I beseech thee, show me thy glory.

¹⁹ And he said, I will make all my goodness pass before thee, and I will proclaim the name of the LORD before thee; and will be gracious to whom I will be gracious, and will show mercy on whom I will show mercy.

²⁰ And God said, Thou cannot see my face: for there shall no man see me, and live.

²¹ And the LORD said, Behold, there is a place by me, and thou shall stand upon a rock:

²² And it shall come to pass, while I pass by, that I will put thee in a cleft of the rock, and will cover thee with my hand while I pass by:

²³ And I will take away mine hand, and thou shall see my back: but my face shall not be seen.

You can see from this passage of scripture that God has a face, a hand and a back. I will guarantee you that God also has the rest of His body. God is a Spirit Body Being.

Isaiah 6:1 In the year that king Uzziah died I saw also the LORD sitting upon a throne, high and lifted up, and his train filled the temple.

It takes a body to <u>sit</u> on a throne.

Genesis 3:8 And they heard the voice of the LORD God walking in the garden in the cool of the day: and Adam and his wife hid themselves from the presence of the LORD God amongst the trees of the garden.

God must have a Spirit Body if He is **walking** in the garden.

Luke 16:19-24 There was a certain rich man, which was clothed in purple and fine linen, and fared sumptuously every day:

²⁰ And there was a certain beggar named Lazarus, which was laid at his gate, full of sores,

²¹ And desiring to be fed with the crumbs which fell from the rich man's table: moreover the dogs came and licked his sores.

²² And it came to pass, that the beggar died, and was carried by the angels into Abraham's bosom: the rich man also died, and was buried;

²³ And in hell he lift up his eyes, being in torments, and seeing Abraham afar off, and Lazarus in his bosom.

²⁴ And he cried and said, Father Abraham, have mercy on me, and send Lazarus, that he may dip the tip of his finger in water, and cool my tongue; for I am tormented in this flame.

These two people died and were buried. Lazarus was carried by the angels into Abraham's bosom, which was the place people went before Jesus carried them with Him to Heaven. The angels are also going to carry our spirits to Heaven when we leave this earth.

The rich man died and his earthly body was buried, but his spirit went into hell. The Bible does not tell us why one went to Abraham's bosom and the other went to hell. I do know it had nothing to do with how much money each of them had.

We can plainly see that the spirits of these two men, after they had died and passed into eternity, had eyes, fingers, and a tongue. I will guarantee you that they also had the rest of their spirit bodies. We are created in the image of God. I believe our spirit body is probably a lot smaller than the Spirit Body of God.

The word likeness in verse 26 means to resemble, to operate like We do. Now the question is, how does God operate? BY SPEAKING. How did Jesus operate when He was on the earth? BY SPEAKING. How are we suppose to operate? BY SPEAKING.

When God created man, He gave him authority over all the earth, over fish, fowl, cattle, and every animal and every creature that moves upon the earth. In other words, God gave man authority over the entire earth and everything in it. God did not however, give people dominion over other people.

Every person on this earth has **an area of authority** and it includes their own life and family. People are to exercise dominion over their own life. You are supposed to dominate your area of authority, with your words.

How does a king dominate his kingdom? By using his words to cause change.

How did my mother dominate her house when my brother and I were growing up? She would use her words to effect change. Oh, I forgot to mention, she had a fly swatter in her hand while she was speaking her words of dominance.

Proverbs 18:21 Your tongue has the power of life and death over you: and you shall live by the words that come out of your mouth.

Every person has the power to create with their words, just like God does; only our area of authority is a lot smaller than His.

When you say something about yourself and believe it, those words will create what you have spoken, into your life.

After Genesis 1:26 where God gives dominion of the earth to man, nothing can happen in this earth unless a person in authority commands it to happen. God only moves in this earth, by faith filled words, which are spoken by a person in authority.

God will also move if we pray and ask Him for something, that it is His will for us to have and if we believe we receive it, when we ask. Mark 11:24

Everyone has the authority to **Bless themselves or curse themselves.** Every time you say something about yourself and **believe** what you are saying, you are **either Blessing yourself, or cursing yourself.** Get the words that come out of your mouth under control. Be careful what you say about yourself or anyone under your spiritual authority.

James 3:10 Out of the same mouth proceeds blessing and cursing. My brethren, this should not be.

I keep a roll of **duct tape** by my pulpit at all times. I even carry it with me when I do conferences. I do not actually put it over the mouths of people, although there have been times when I was tempted to do so. They will get a piece of tape on their Bible to remind them that they said something wrong about themselves. I tell everyone to **keep their mouth shut** after I pray for them and speak over them concerning their healing or finances. When I speak over people, under my spiritual authority, they will get what they want or need every time because **what I say will happen**.

> **James 3:2-6 For in many things we offend all. If any man offend not with his words, the same is a mature man, and able also to control the whole body.**

The Bible tells us that a Christian, who controls his words and does not curse himself, is considered to be a mature believer. A Christian who does not control his words and who does curse himself is considered to be an immature Christian. I call people, who cannot control their words, **Baby Christians** and it does not matter how long they have been saved, or how much of the Bible they can quote.

The Lord's brother, James, is describing the power of the tongue.

> ³ **Behold, we put bits in the horses' mouth that they may obey us; and we turn about their whole body.**

Your tongue is little, but it is **The Instrument of Authority** in your life, just like the bit is the instrument of authority with a horse.

> ⁴ **Behold also the ships, which though they be so great, and are driven of fierce winds, yet are they turned about with a very small rudder, whithersoever the Captain turns.**

YOUR TONGUE CAN TURN YOUR LIFE AROUND!

> ⁵ **Even so the tongue is a little member, and boast great things. Behold, how great a matter a little fire kindles**

> ⁶ **And the tongue is a fire, a world of iniquity: so is the tongue among our members, that it defiles the whole body, and sets on fire the course of nature; and it is set on fire of hell.**

Your tongue has the power to change the natural course of events in your body and in your life. For example, your tongue can cause you to feel young or old. Your tongue can also lengthen or shorten your life and cause you to be sick or well, or rich or poor.

Use your words to make good things happen in your life
By speaking Blessings over Yourself.

Speak Blessings over your family, your job, car, house, computer and your dog. If you happen to be a cat person, I suppose you could speak over your cat.

Sometimes God will tell a person what to say to make things happen. Case in point, God was going to raise up Israel and bring them back from captivity, but what He wanted to do needed to be spoken by someone in authority. That was the Prophet Ezekiel. God carried him in the spirit out to the valley of dry bones and told him what to say.

Ezekiel 37:1-10 The hand of the LORD was upon me, and carried me out in the spirit of the LORD, and set me down in the midst of the valley which was full of bones,

² And caused me to pass by them round about: and, behold, there were very many in the open valley; and, lo, they were very dry.

³ And he said unto me, Son of man, can these bones live? And I answered, O Lord GOD, thou knows.

⁴ Again he said unto me, Prophesy upon these bones, and say unto them, O ye dry bones, hear the word of the LORD.

⁵ Thus says the Lord GOD unto these bones; Behold, I will cause breath to enter into you, and ye shall live:

⁶ And I will lay sinews upon you, and will bring up flesh upon you, and cover you with skin, and put breath in you, and ye shall live; and ye shall know that I am the LORD.

⁷ So I prophesied as I was commanded: and as I prophesied, there was a noise, and behold a shaking, and the bones came together, bone to his bone.

⁸ And when I beheld, lo, the sinews and the flesh came up upon them, and the skin covered them above: but there was no breath in them.

⁹ Then said he unto me, Prophesy unto the wind, prophesy, son of man, and say to the wind, Thus says the Lord GOD; Come from

the four winds, O breath, and breathe upon these slain, that they may live.

¹⁰ So I prophesied as he commanded me, and the breath came into them, and they lived, and stood up upon their feet, an exceeding great army.

If you are in a situation ask God what to say. He will tell you.

You must speak something, either good or bad and believe it will happen and not doubt in your heart, in order to effect change. Example, if you say I get sick every year when the flu comes around and believe it, you will get sick. You have cursed yourself and created sickness in your body with your words. You have given the devil a legal right to bring sickness to you and he most certainly will do just that. Or, if you say, I can never seem to get ahead, or I can't afford a new car, or I will never get over this cold, you have just cursed yourself. Or, if you say something really dumb like my kids are sick all the time they will be sick all the time. Or if you say my kids have a hard time learning in school, you have just cursed the learning process of your children.

Faith Filled Blessing

If you are waiting for God to Bless you, you are going to wait a long time, unless you, or someone in authority, speaks a faith filled Blessing over you. A faith filled Blessing is a Blessing spoken by a person in authority, who absolutely knows that what they say will happen. A Blessing spoken without faith will get no results. In other words, nothing happens.

A person who imparts the Blessing over himself or another person must believe that what he says is absolutely going to happen, in order to get results.

Genesis 1:28 And God blessed them, and God said unto them, Be fruitful, and multiply, and replenish the earth, and subdue it: and have dominion over the fish of the sea, and over the fowl of the air, and over every living thing that moves upon the earth.

These are what we call **First Words**. The first thing man ever heard was God speaking The Blessing over him. This was and still is God's will for all mankind.

God has absolute faith in His Words

The purpose, for The Blessing that God spoke over Adam and his wife, was to empower them to dominate the earth with their words and to spread the Garden of Eden over the entire earth. When they sinned, God took away The Blessing and the Curse came in and replaced The Blessing.

Genesis 9:1 And God Blessed Noah and his sons, and said unto them, Be fruitful, and multiply, and replenish the earth.

After the flood, God had to start over again with Noah and his sons. He Blessed them with the Same Blessing He had spoken over Adam and his wife. This Blessing also had the same purpose, to empower Noah and his sons to dominate the world and to create and spread the Garden of Eden over the entire world.

Noah spoke The Blessing over two of his sons and cursed the other son.

Only one of Noah's sons, Shem, continued in The Blessing so God had to look for someone else.

Genesis 12:1-3 Now the LORD had said unto Abram, Get thee out of thy country, and from thy kindred, and from thy father's house, unto a land that I will show thee: ² And I will make of thee a great nation, and I will bless thee, and make thy name great; and thou shall be a blessing: ³ And I will bless them that bless thee, and curse him that curses thee: and in thee shall all families of the earth be blessed.

Genesis 14:18-20 And Melchizedek king of Salem brought forth bread and wine: and he was the priest of the Most High God. ¹⁹ And he blessed him, and said, Blessed be Abram of the most high God, possessor of heaven and earth: ²⁰ And blessed be the most high God, which hath delivered your enemies into thy hand. And he gave him tithes of all.

Even though God had said He was going to Bless Abraham, it had to be voice activated by a person in authority. That was Melchizedek, Priest of The Most High God. **Notice that Abraham also gave his tithe to the Priest who spoke The Blessing over him. I do the same thing.**

A person's <u>Pastor or Priest</u> has the authority to speak The Blessing over people under his or her ministry.

Genesis 27:27-29 And Jacob came near his father, Isaac and kissed him: and he smelled the smell of his clothes, and blessed him, and said, See, the smell of my son is as the smell of a field which the LORD HATH BLESSED: [28] Therefore God give thee of the dew of heaven, and the fatness of the earth, and plenty of corn and wine: [29] Let people serve thee, and nations bow down to thee: be lord over thy brethren, and let thy mother's sons bow down to thee: cursed be every one that curses thee, and blessed be he that blesses thee.

The Blessing was so important to Jacob that he was willing to risk his life to have it spoken over him by his father. Is The Blessing, spoken by a father, any less important today than it was then? Most assuredly, it is not less important today than it was in the days of Jacob. Our children are very successful because we speak The Blessing over them. The most important thing that parents can do for their children is to speak Blessings over them.

Why do you think the Jewish people have such successful children? It is because they speak The Blessing of Abraham over them on a regular basis.

Jacob esteemed The Blessing and
we should do the same thing.

A person's <u>Parents</u> have the authority to speak

The Blessing over their children.

Ask your parents to speak
The Blessing of Abraham over you.

Genesis 28:1-4 And Isaac called Jacob, and blessed him, and charged him, and said unto him, Thou shall not take a wife of the daughters of Canaan. ² Arise go to Padanaram, to the house of Bethuel thy mother's father; and take thee a wife from thence of the daughters of Laban thy mother's brother. ³ And God Almighty bless thee, and make thee fruitful, and multiply thee, that thou may be a multitude of people; ⁴ And give thee the <u>Blessing of Abraham</u>, to thee, and to thy seed with thee; that thou may inherit

**the land wherein thou art a stranger, which
God gave unto Abraham.**

Here Isaac is speaking the actual Blessing of Abraham
over Jacob. This is one of the Blessings that Jewish people
speak over their sons. They speak The Blessing of Rachel
and Leah over their daughters. I guarantee you that Isaac
learned about imparting The Blessing from his father,
Abraham, who undoubtedly spoke The Blessing over him.

The Blessing of Abraham empowered Jacob for success
and it will do the same thing for you.

You Can Immediately
Empower Your Children For Success

When I got a revelation of Isaac Blessing Jacob, I spoke
The Blessing of Abraham over my own son and his whole
life changed. When Jeffrey was little he would sit on my
lap and I would say, "You are a good boy and you are
smart." He would say, "I'm a big boy." I would say, "Yes,
you are a big boy. You are also a good boy and you are
smart." He grew up to be a good boy and he is very smart.

Every time my son began a new semester in college,
I would speak over him and say, "You are smart and you

have a supernatural knowledge of the material you are learning." You can do the same thing with your children starting right now and it does not matter what their age is. The words of the Faith Filled Blessing you speak over them will change their life. I guarantee it.

Have a Blessing Ceremony in your home, no matter what age your children are. Line up the children and grandchildren (if you have them) place your right hand on their head and speak The Blessing over them.

What you speak over them will happen!

Say, "I Bless you with The Blessing of Abraham. You will live your entire life in your own Garden of Eden. You are smart and you are a good person. You have a supernatural knowledge of the material you are learning in school. You are very happy, successful, healthy and prosperous. You have favor with God and with people and you will serve the Lord all the days of your life and for eternity in Heaven."

If they are working at a job say, "You have favor with the people you work for and you are a huge Blessing to your boss and the company where you work."

If they have their own business say, "I Bless your business and declare that it is very successful and a Blessing to all of your customers and clients."

Fathers should speak The Faith Filled Blessing over their children, but if there is not a believing Father available, then Mothers can do it.

You can speak Blessings over your children, even if they live a thousand miles away. We do that on a regular basis, with children of people in our church and have seen incredible results.

Mary and I knew a lady, years ago, who was a single mother with two little girls who were classified by the school district as "Being retarded." She prayed and spoke Blessings over the little girls everyday and as they slept at night. They both did very well in school. One of them was valedictorian of her entire high school class the year she graduated.

Every child who is born deserves to have The Blessing spoken over them by the people responsible for bringing them into this world. Can you say Amen to that?

The Spoken Blessing makes a huge difference in the life of a child.

Your words will change the lives of your children.

Pastors, please encourage the parents in your church to speak The Blessing over their children on a regular basis.

Genesis 48:9 And Joseph said unto his father, Jacob, They are my sons, whom God hath given me in this place. And he said, Bring them, I pray thee, unto me, and I will bless them.

Jacob had absolute faith in The Spoken Blessing

Jacob spoke a Blessing over all of his children and grandchildren before he died. You can be sure that he knew his authority to do so and that he also had faith in his words.

The Priestly Blessing

Numbers 6:22-27 And the LORD spoke unto Moses, saying, [23] Speak unto Aaron and unto his sons, who were also priests, saying, This

is how you shall bless the children of Israel, saying unto them, ²⁴ The LORD bless thee, and keep thee: ²⁵ The LORD make his face shine upon thee, and be gracious unto thee: ²⁶ The LORD lift up his countenance upon thee, and give you peace. ²⁷ And they shall put my name upon the children of Israel, and I will bless them.

God commanded Moses to teach the Priests how to speak The Blessing, **Word for Word**, over the people and said that when they do this, He would Bless them. This was not a suggestion, it was a commandment, just like the 10 commandments are not 10 suggestions, as many, open minded progressive, people want you to think they are.

I believe Pastors should speak this Blessing, Word for Word over the people in their church on a regular basis.

I got a revelation of this, several years ago, and started speaking this Blessing, word for word, over the people in my church, at the end of every service. I know that I have the authority from God to speak this Blessing. I have faith that when I speak it, God will bless the people. I speak Faith Filled Blessings.

Blessings just rained down on the people in our church, both healings and huge financial Blessings. As long as the people in our church were having The Blessing spoken over them, they remained very prosperous. When they left the church they had to learn to operate in their own faith for The Blessing, just like Isaac did after Abraham died. Many of them decreased, after they left our church and some of the people went broke.

If the people in my church would have had a revelation of what was happening when I spoke The Blessing over them, they would have hired armed bodyguards to protect me and doctors to hover over me to make sure I was feeling OK.

If you are decreasing, ask yourself this question. What was I doing and what was going on in my life when I was being Blessed? There is the answer to your situation.

I know that a huge part of our Blessing and our increase is because of the ministry that Mary and I and are connected to. You can believe me when I tell you that we are staying connected to that person.

If you are connected to a ministry where The Blessing is being spoken over you and you are increasing, STAY

THERE! Keith Moore calls this "Your wealthy place."
If you have left and you are decreasing, GO BACK to
where you were being Blessed before and you will be
Blessed again. Make sense? Huh? Don't let pride block
your Blessing and keep you broke.

Mary and I made a mistake of leaving our wealthy
place and we decreased. When we realized we were in the
wrong place we immediately packed up and went back.
We began to increase again very quickly.

I inquired of the Lord as to why so many of the people in our church were receiving such huge financial
Blessings. He showed me three separate visions of me telling people that God was going to Bless them financially
and it happened exactly as I had spoken.

There have also been so many other cases where exactly what I had spoken over people happened, just like I
said it would. People call me to speak over situations and
they always get what they want or need.

The key to this is that the person speaking The
Blessing, over someone else, must have the authority to
do so and absolute faith that what they say will come to
pass. They must speak a Faith Filled Blessing. Otherwise,

they are just speaking empty words that will produce no results.

Several years ago my Mother had heart by-pass surgery at Pittsburgh University Hospital. She was taken into recovery, three times her normal size, due to fluid retention from the IVs. About the forth day or so, the nurse came into the waiting room and said, "We are losing her. Her vital signs are quickly going down and if you want to see her before she dies, you should come in right away." As we could only go in two at a time, my brother and his wife went first. They came out in five minutes and Jerry shook his head at me as if to say, there is no hope.

As Mary and I followed the nurse down the hall toward Mom's room, The Lord spoke into my spirit in an audible voice and said, "You are the oldest son".

We went into the room and in a loud voice I said, "You will not die. You will live out your life. I command the spirit of death to leave you and these vital signs to go up, right now, in the Name of Jesus. Doctors and nurses from all over the area came rushing in to find out what was causing all of the noise and commotion. We all stood there for several minutes, with no one saying a word.

Everyone (except Mary and I) watched in disbelief as the gages, which relay information regarding the vital signs, starting moving up. Finally one of the doctors said, "She is out of the woods." She lived another three years, with a good quality of life and then went to be with Jesus. The last two weeks of her life on this earth, she was responsible for bringing a lady, she had known for years, to The Lord.

A king will rule his kingdom with his words. We rule our area of authority, which is our kingdom, with our faith filled words.

I think we need to learn more about our authority and the power of our words. Faith filled words, spoken <u>within our area of authority,</u> will change situations or circumstances.

Romans 5:17 states that we are called to reign in life by Christ Jesus and the way we reign, within our area of authority, is by our words.

People in my church and our ministry partners have been Blessed and healed and have greatly increased over the years, because I do have faith in my authority to speak The Blessing of Abraham and prosperity and healing over them. I know my area of authority and you should also.

If you do not yet have faith enough to receive the Blessing of Abraham on your own, connect with someone who has the faith to speak it over you. You can walk in their Blessing until your own faith increases for The Blessing. That is what I did and you can believe me, it works.

Have the Faith Filled Blessing spoken over you.

I am staying Blessed and increasing because the person speaking over me and my ministry has faith in their authority to speak The Blessing. I know they also have faith in their words. I fully intend to stay connected to this person. I have his Blessing and his Anointing. I intend to keep them both while my faith is increasing and that is for as long as I am on this earth. I will never get out from under **That Man's Blessing**.

Stay connected to The Blessing!

A person who just speaks The Blessing, without faith in their words, will get no results. Make sure the person speaking over you has the faith to do it.

1 Samuel 1:17 Then Eli answered and said to Hannah, Go in peace: and the God of Israel

grant thee thy petition that thou hast asked of him.

I think the relationship between Eli the Priest and Hannah, is something we need to take a look at. There is something very important here that the church has missed. Does anyone know why Hannah, who had been praying and asking God to open her womb and give her a son for years, only received the answer to her prayer when the Priest spoke that The God of Israel would grant her the petition she was asking? Apparently, the Priest had the authority to speak over the people in those days.

Hannah was <u>expecting a baby boy, before she conceived,</u> because she had faith in the words that the Priest had spoken over her.

1 Samuel 2:20-21 And Eli blessed Elkanah and his wife, and said, The LORD give thee seed of this woman for the loan which is lent to the LORD. And they went unto their own home. [21] And the LORD visited Hannah, so that she conceived, and bare three sons and two daughters. And the child Samuel grew before the LORD.

Eli spoke a Faith Filled Blessing

Eli spoke another Blessing over Hannah and her husband, and she had five more children. This was a woman who could not conceive when she was young and she was now advanced in years. The Blessing spoken over Hannah by Eli, the Priest, caused her to multiply, which is what The Blessing does.

How about the New Testament?

Philippians 4:19 But my God shall supply all your need according to his riches in glory by Christ Jesus.

This is The Blessing Paul spoke over the Philippians who had financially supported his ministry. I would say that Paul knew he had the authority to speak this Blessing. He also had faith in his words, or he would not have done it. As far as I know, Paul did not speak a financial Blessing over anyone else.

I would surmise from this also that **any minister,** that you support financially, would have the **same authority (as Paul)** to speak a financial Blessing over you, if they understand this authority and have the faith to do it.

I would also imagine that, after this book comes out, every minister in the country will be speaking The Blessing over his or her financial supporters. That is the way it should be. I want all of God's people to have The Blessing spoken over them.

<u>A Minister of God's Word</u>, whom you support financially, definitely has the authority to speak The Blessing over you. Just make sure that the person, speaking over you, has the faith to do it or you will see no results.

You Can Bless Yourself.

Say good things about yourself all day long, everyday. Your life will eventually conform to the words you speak about yourself.

Some examples are, "I am losing weight, I have lots of friends, people like me, I have a great job, my life is wonderful" and so on.

You can even improve your intelligence by saying, "I am smart and getting smarter every day." Try that and I guarantee that you will notice a difference after a few months.

> Luke 24:50-51 And he led them out as far as to Bethany, and he lifted up his hands, and blessed them. [51] And it came to pass, while he blessed them, he was parted from them, and carried up into heaven.

Jesus had absolute faith in His Words.

This is what we call **Last Words**. The last thing Jesus ever spoke on the earth was The Blessing and as you remember, the First Words God spoke to man were The Blessing.

THE SPOKEN BLESSING IS VERY IMPORTANT!

Say out loud, "I am Blessed because the Blessing has been spoken over me by a person in authority to do so. I have spoken The Blessing over myself and The Blessing of Abraham is my inheritance. I believe I receive The Blessing of Abraham in the Wonderful Name of Jesus."

Say out loud 100 times a day, "The Blessing of Abraham is my inheritance and I believe I receive The Blessing."

Share this with everyone you know who needs The Blessing spoken over them, or who have children who need to be empowered for success.

Give a copy of this book to your Pastor and after they have read it, ask Him, or Her to speak The Blessing over you.

If your parents are still alive, give them a copy of this book and after they have read it, ask them to speak The Blessing over you.

Chapter 4

THE BLESSING CONNECTOR

Honor The Lord and Connect yourself to The Blessing at the same time.

<u>Leviticus 27:30</u> And all the tithe of the land, whether of the seed of the land, or of the fruit of the tree, is the Lord's: it is holy unto the Lord.

<u>Numbers 18:26</u> Thus speak unto the Levites, and say unto them, When ye take of the children of Israel the tithes which I have given you from them for your inheritance, then ye

shall offer up an heave offering of it for the Lord, even a tenth part of the tithe.

Malachi 3:10 Bring ye all the tithes into the storehouse, that there may be meat in mine house, and prove me now herewith, says the LORD of hosts, if I will not open you the windows of heaven, and pour you out a blessing, that there shall not be room enough to receive it.

The Tithe is the Blessing Connector.

Proverbs 3:9-10 Honor the LORD with thy substance, and with the first fruits of all your increase: ¹⁰ So shall thy barns be filled with plenty, and thy presses shall burst out with new wine.

You do not pay the tithe. You bring the tithe.

Talk is cheap, it is the tithe that honors God.

No one is too poor to tithe.

Not tithing is robbing God. Don't be a robber.

People who do not tithe should not expect The Blessing of Abraham to come upon them and they should not expect God to Bless their finances.

Tithing removes the curse from your finances.

If you do not tithe, 100% of your money will not be enough. However, if you do tithe, the 90% that is yours to keep will be more than enough.

When Abraham lifted up his hand to God he was saying, I have brought my tithe and I expect God alone to Bless me. And He did. Abraham did not want anyone else, other than God, to be able to say that they had made him rich.

Genesis 28:20-22 And Jacob vowed a vow, saying, If God will be with me, and will keep me in this way that I go, and will give me bread to eat, and raiment to put on,

21 So that I come again to my father's house in peace; then shall the LORD be my God:

22 And this stone, which I have set for a pillar, shall be God's house: and of all that thou

shalt give me I will surely give the <u>tenth</u> unto thee.

Jacob made a vow to tithe and became rich, even though his father in law cheated him and lowered his wages ten times. He actually became so rich that he could not contain all of it; he had to divide his goods into two groups.

When a person makes a decision or a vow to tithe, God makes a decision to Bless them. Make a vow to tithe and see what happens.

Set aside a special time to tithe because tithing is much more important than just writing out a check and putting it in the basket at church, or mailing it in.

Mary and I tithe first thing every Monday morning. I will wake Mary up and say, come on, let's get our tithe going. We are excited about getting our tithe ready.

We will count up every penny that has come into our church and ministry and then write out the tithe check, which is exactly ten percent, and put it into the envelope.

We then pray and have communion over our tithe. We say, "Father God, Your Word says to bring the entire tithe into the storehouse that there may be food in Your House and that is what we are doing. You said that we should test You, if You will not open the windows of Heaven and pour us out a Blessing that there will not be room enough to receive it. That You will rebuke the devourer for us. You will cause people to call us Blessed. We expect You to do all of that Lord, in the Name of Jesus."

"And Father God, our tithe connects us to an Anointed person who is living and ministering in The Fullness of The Blessing of Abraham and we have his Blessing, his Anointing and his favor."

"And Father God, Your Word also says that we should Honor You with the first fruits of all our increase. Lord we do honor You with our tithe. You said, that You will fill our bank accounts, which is our barns and cause overflow in our lives. We expect that, and we thank You for that in the Name of Jesus. Amen."

I then get in the car with the envelope and my dog of course. We take the check to the post office and mail it and this is all done before 9 AM.

We do not want our tithe, which is Holy to God, in our house. It belongs to God and we want it out and on the way as quickly as possible. One day I put it in the mailbox and was bothered all day because I knew The Lord's money was sitting out there waiting for the mailman. God's money should not be sitting out there in the hot sun. Is that silly? Not when you take tithing as seriously as we do and when you have a revelation of how important the tithe is to God.

We have a revelation that our tithe connects us to The Blessing.

Connect to a Blessed Person's Blessing

The person we tithe to is Blessed and Anointed and that same Blessing that is on him is on us and we also have his Anointing. The tithe connects us to him just like Abraham was connected to Melchizedek, through the tithe.

If I ever come face to face with this man, I will tell him, I have your Blessing and your Anointing and I thank you for it.

I told Brother Hagin, face to face, "I got saved reading the back of one of your little books." He just looked up at me and said, "Praise God."

Get in The Blessing Line!

In order for the ministry to increase, that we tithe to, we must increase, and we do. In order for us to increase, our partners must increase and they do. It is a down the line effect and it is God's method of increasing everyone who is connected to The Blessing. Are you in a Blessing Increase that increase line?

The Blessing comes through me to my family, people in my church and ministry partners. Everyone who is connected to me through the tithe is connected to The Blessing.

Our obligation is to bring the Tithe.

God's obligation is to:

1. Open the Windows of Heaven and Pour us out a Blessing that there is not room enough to receive it. Malachi 3:10

2. Rebuke the devourer for our sake so he will not spoil what we have been working on. Malachi 3:11

3. Cause people to call us Blessed. Malachi 3:12

4. Fill our barns (bank accounts) with plenty. Proverbs 3:10

5. Cause our presses to burst out with new wine (overflow). Proverbs 3:10

6. Surround us with favor. Psalms 5:12

We are supposed to test God to see if He will do it. Every time you bring the tithe say, "Lord, this is a test".

If you tithe you have a right to test God about your finances. I do.

One day, when Mary and I were in Bible College, she was balancing our checkbook. As she finished, she announced that our balance was a grand total of 58 cents, which was all we had left in our bank account. We had no money coming in and we had rent and tuition due in a few days.

That evening in church as the offering bucket was being passed around I took out my wallet to get out a dollar. All I had left in there was one 10 dollar bill. I took it out and Mary said to me, "I hope you are hearing from the Lord." I dropped it into the bucket and it floated down in super slow motion. That was the largest offering we ever gave. We had given all we had.

The next morning I was reading in my One Year Bible and I read Proverbs 10:9-10 **Honor the LORD with thy substance, and with the first fruits of all your increase: ¹⁰ So shall thy barns be filled with plenty, and thy presses shall burst out with new wine.**

I put down my Bible and stood up and said, "Lord, I have given You all I have. I have nothing more to give. It is Your turn to Bless me, I am all done. I have nothing left to give; now You Bless my finances and do it right now."

That afternoon our finances opened up and we had plenty of money to finish Bible College and we were even able to help other people with their tuition. God's Word works. If you tithe, you can make a demand that God Bless your finances.

God only wants the First and the Best 10%. In order for the tithe to be the true tithe it must be taken out first, not after the bills are paid.

My friend, Pastor Calvin Hooper, from Household of Faith Church, in Round Rock, Texas, tells the story in his book, "8 Essentials For Following Jesus," of a lady bringing her offering to the Pastor. She gave him a check for $50 and asked, if her gift was satisfactory." He replied, "If it represents you." She asked for her check back and left.

She came back a few days later with a check for $5,000. Again, she asked if her gift was satisfactory. The Pastor again replied, "If it represents you." Once again she asked for her check back and left.

She returned again in a few days and handed the Pastor a check for $50,000 and said, "This gift does represent me and I am happy to give it."

Your tithes, offerings and gifts to the Lord represent you, each and every time that you give. God gave us the gift of His Dear Son Jesus, and this gift to us represented Almighty God, Himself.

Genesis 4:3-5 And in process of time it came to pass, that Cain brought of the fruit of the ground an offering unto the Lord.

⁴ And Abel, he also brought of the firstlings of his flock and of the fat thereof. And

the LORD had respect unto Abel and to his offering:

⁵ But unto Cain and to his offering he had not respect. And Cain was very wroth, and his countenance fell.

The Bible does not say that Cain's offering was the **first** fruits and so it was not acceptable to The Lord.

Abel's offering was the **firstlings** of his flock which means it was taken out first and it was the best. This offering was acceptable to The Lord.

Abraham knew about tithing and brought his tithe to the Priest 400 years before Moses commanded the people to tithe.

A person who tithes is a person who trusts God to provide for them.

God looks at a person who tithes as being trustworthy.

God holds nothing back from a person who tithes.

You bring the tithe and God will open the windows of heaven and pour.

Tithing positions me under the windows of Heaven.

You make a quality decision to tithe and the minute the first tithe leaves your hand you can demand that God open the windows of Heaven and pour you out a Blessing that there will not be room enough to receive it. And He will do just that.

Say out loud, "My tithe connects me to The Blessing."

Say out loud, "Because I tithe, I am Blessed with the Blessing of Abraham. The windows of Heaven are open to me. The Blessing is being poured out upon me. The devourer has been rebuked for my sake. People call me Blessed. My bank account is full and my life is overflowing with abundance and good things. Thank You Lord."

Tell all of your friends, who seemed to be cursed in their finances, to read this book.

Chapter 5

FAITH TO RECEIVE THE BLESSING OF ABRAHAM

The Faith of Abraham Activated The Blessing of Abraham in The Life of Abraham.

Abraham walked in each area of the Blessing, as he developed his faith for that part of The Blessing, which God had spoken over him.

God said to Abraham I will Bless you. Then Melchizedek voice activated The Blessing by speaking over him. However, Abraham only walked in The Blessing that had been given to him according to his faith. The law of faith is that we receive everything from God, only according to our faith, and that also applied to Abraham who is called the Father of faith.

The Blessing of Abraham has already been given to us, through Jesus. We will only live in it according to our faith, just like Abraham did.

All of God's people have also been given healing and prosperity, but we will only be able to receive them, according to our faith.

Matthew 9:29 Then Jesus touched their eyes, saying, "According to your faith it will be it unto you."

As far as I am concerned, this is the key verse, in the Bible, which explains why some people receive what God has already provided and some do not. **God never moves according to the needs of any person.** God does not heal people because they need to be healed, or provide for people because they need money to pay their bills. He also does not give food to people, because they are hungry.

God only moves in our lives <u>according</u> to our faith

But the good news is that you can increase your faith, for whatever you want or need, and receive it from God every time, if you know how.

Everyone wants to believe that they are living by faith and that they have great faith. The truth of the matter is you can only tell whether or not a person has faith by their **results**. If you see results you know a person has faith.

John Wesley said, many years ago, "The devil has given the church a substitute for faith, which is so much like faith, that few people can tell the difference." He called it mental assent. I call it head faith. How can you tell the difference? BY RESULTS.

So many people have faith in their head and are waiting for things to happen. I hate to tell you this, but for many years, that was me. Not anymore. If I am not getting results, right away, I am working on increasing my faith.

God is not slow concerning His promises. The minute you connect in faith for what you want, or need, your answer is coming toward you at the speed of light.

Don't get caught in the trap of standing in faith that you do not have. People die and go broke doing this.

Another trap is waiting on God's timing to get results. God's timing is always **right now**. God is not going to make you wait for healing, or for The Blessing, anymore than He would make you wait for salvation, when you receive Jesus as your Savior, or for forgiveness, when you repent.

Believing God's Word in your head is good, but it does not produce results. Only true faith, or as Paul described it to Timothy, unfeigned faith, will bring results.

True Faith is Believing in your Heart

Two things are necessary for true faith:

1. Knowing God's will.

2. Making a decision to believe God's Word.

Faith will also overcome time, nature, situations and circumstances.

Several years ago, I called Mary into the office and said, "I know why we are not prospering financially." She said, "Why." I said, "Because I do not have enough faith for our finances." She looked at me and said, "Well, **get the faith**" and turned around and walked away. I yelled to her, "I am going to."

When you admit that you do not have the faith to receive what you need from God, you empower yourself to increase your faith. Everything then becomes possible in your life.

I have had faith to pray the prayer of faith and speak over sick people since about three weeks after I got saved. For the last 13 years or so, I have had faith to speak The Blessing over the people in my church, to pray the prayer of faith, speak Blessings over their finances and for their healing. I even had faith for my own healing. I did not however, have faith for my own finances, or for The Blessing, in my own life.

I embarked on a very intensive program to increase my faith for our finances and The Blessing and I am very happy to tell you that <u>God's Word Works</u>.

You are where you are, in every area of your life, because of where your faith is in that area. Many people do not know that faith in one area will not help you in another area. For instance, faith for healing will not help your finances and the other way around. You must have faith in each area. Abraham had faith for abundance right away, but it took him over 24 years to increase his faith for a child with his 90 year old wife.

I realized that there were several areas where I needed to increase my faith. That is just what I did and anyone else can do the same thing.

Hebrews 11:1 Now faith is the confident expectation of things you cannot yet see. Faith is expecting what you do not yet have and cannot even see. When you are expecting something, you are excited, so as Keith Moore said, "Excitement is the faith gage." The higher your level of excitement about something, the more faith you have. Kenneth Hagin said, "The Word that excites you is the Word that will work for you." If you are getting excited about The Blessing, you are getting close to having The Blessing of Abraham operating in your life.

Jesus said, "Where is your faith?" There are different levels of faith:

A person who is caught out in the middle of the sea, during a storm, who has "No faith," will drown.

If that same person has "Little faith," he might survive.

If that person has "Faith," he will put his head down, turn the boat into the wind and fight his way through the storm. He will eventually survive.

However, if that same person has "Great faith," he will "Speak the Word only," to the storm, tell it to stop, and go through on a calm sea.

I will never again fight my way through any storm, situation, or circumstance and neither should you. Speak the Word in faith, believing that what you say will happen, and everything will change.

<u>Jesus never prayed for a sick person</u>. A person with faith does not ask God to heal someone who is sick, or even themselves. Faith speaks to the sickness and the devil causing the oppression and tells it to leave, in the Name of Jesus.

Faith believes in your heart that
God will do what He said He will do.

God picked Abraham and his seed for The Blessing. Absolutely anyone, who is the seed of Abraham, can walk in the fullness of the Blessing of Abraham, if they will just increase their faith for it. This Blessing is available to you. You are supposed to have it and it is a shame that so many of God's people are living without it. I, as well as some others, are determined that is going to change.

Abraham was Blessed by God's promise, but he had to received it by faith. The Blessing is also promised to us, as the seed of Abraham. We must also receive it by faith, just like Abraham did.

Without faith, Abraham would have had the promise of The Blessing, but would not have walked in it.

People who have faith for The Blessing are Blessed like Abraham.

85% of the Jewish people are walking in the Blessing of Abraham.

Less than 1% of Christians are walking in the Blessing of Abraham. What is the difference? The Jewish people have faith for the Blessing of Abraham and most Christians don't.

Jews do not toil to earn a living because they have faith for The Blessing of Abraham and faith in the Blessing. Check out the dish washers, ditch diggers, lawn care workers, construction crews, house painters, or other people working out in the hot sun. You will not find any Jewish people out there, or at least, very few. They <u>own</u> the construction companies, they <u>own</u> the restaurants. They <u>own</u> the banks, the Television networks, the newspapers and the movie studios. They are doctors and lawyers and even though they are only 2% of the American population, they control over 50% of the money.

Why is this? Is it because they are God's chosen people? Yes, they are God's chosen people and they are told that from the time they are little children, <u>BUT SO ARE WE.</u> We are born again and most of them are not, so we have a better covenant. The Jewish people believe that The Blessing of Abraham is their heritage and it is, but it is also our heritage, as born again believers.

The Jewish people **HAVE FAITH FOR THE BLESSING OF ABRAHAM.**

WE CAN LIVE LIKE THEY LIVE IF WE WILL JUST HAVE FAITH FOR THE BLESSING LIKE THEY DO.

There is plenty to go around for all of God's people.

It has been God's will from the foundation of the world for <u>all</u> of His people to walk in His Blessing, but we must develop our faith to do it.

Faith is the switch that turns on The Blessing of Abraham in your life.

Caleb said in Joshua 14:12, "Now give me this mountain that the Lord said was mine." True faith makes a demand on God's Word. You should also make a **demand** according to what God promised Abraham and his seed, which is you.

True faith also, <u>never</u> makes a demand on people, which is looking to man, instead of God. That will remove The Blessing and bring a curse on your finances. Jeremiah 17:5.

You do not need to ask God for The Blessing of Abraham because it has already been given to you. You just need to increase your faith to possess it, the same as you would increase your faith to receive healing, or anything else.

It takes faith to possess what God has already given us.

God gave us The Blessing by promise,
we live in it by faith.

The Blessing of Abraham, like everything else from God,
is appropriated by faith.

Exodus 20:1-3 And God spoke all these words, saying,

²I am the LORD thy God, which have brought thee out of the land of Egypt, out of the house of bondage.

³Thou shall have no other gods before me.

Jeremiah 17:5-8 Thus says the LORD; <u>Cursed be the man that trusts in man</u>, and makes flesh his arm, and whose heart departs from the LORD.

⁶For he shall be like the heath in the desert, and shall not see when good cometh; but shall inhabit the parched places in the wilderness, in a salt land and not inhabited.

⁷ Blessed is the man that trusts in the LORD, and whose hope the LORD is.

⁸ For he shall be as a tree planted by the waters, and that spreads out her roots by the river, and shall not see when heat cometh, but her leaf shall be green; and shall not be careful in the year of drought, neither shall cease from yielding fruit.

In order to be eligible to live in The Blessing we must get to the point where all of our trust is in God, not other people and definitely not ourselves, to provide for us, or to heal us.

We go to the doctors, who treat the symptoms and we take the medicine, but we depend on God alone to heal us. We go to our jobs, get paychecks, social security checks and pensions, but we depend on God alone to provide for us. God does not want us to put our trust in anyone else, for our provisions, not even ourselves.

If for any reason, you make anything or anyone, other than God, your source for anything, whether it is finances or healing, as far as God is concerned, they have become your total source of supply. He will step back and allow them to provide for you. You will then be limited to what they have the ability to do for you, or provide for you.

If the doctor cannot cure you, you will die. If you do not make enough money at your job to pay your bills, you will live in poverty. Make God your total source of supply and He will heal you and meet all of your need, according to His riches in glory, by Christ Jesus.

Become Blessing Minded

In order to possess the Blessing of Abraham that God has given us, we must go through a process of renewing our mind, until we get to the point, where we become, as Brother Copeland so perfectly puts it, **Blessing Minded**.

The Blessing of Abraham should be on your mind, coming out of your mouth and going into your ears, day and night, until you are walking in the fullness of it. If you are willing to do this for as long as it takes, it won't take long.

Saying, "I believe I have The Blessing, or The Blessing of Abraham is my inheritance," over and over, day after day, week after week, month after month plants the seed. The seed will grow while you sleep and get up and go about your business. You do not know, cannot know and do not need to know, how it grows. The fruit it will produce is The Blessing of Abraham. Don't dig up that seed by speaking or hearing bad words. Mark 4:3-32 Jesus also said, "Be careful what you hear." That is so important because you will become like the people you listen to.

It can take some time for positive confession to take root and start growing in your heart, so keep speaking for as long as it takes.

Faith must be released and speaking God's Word, releases your faith.

What is your **determination factor?** You must become **absolutely determined** to have The Fullness of The Blessing for yourself.

> **Romans 12:2 And be not conformed to this world: but be ye transformed by the renewing of your mind, that ye may prove what is that good, and acceptable, and perfect, will of God.**

Creflo Dollar said, "When you get a revelation that The Blessing of Abraham belongs to you, your life will begin to change." He is so right. One day, as we were beginning to get new revelation about The Blessing of Abraham, I said to Mary, "The Blessing of Abraham really does belong to us." She looked at me and said, "It does belong to us." Three days later there was a huge check in the mailbox and our finances were all straightened out. How awesome is that, HUH??

If you are born again
The Blessing of Abraham is your Birthright.

You will know you are on your way to living in The Blessing of Abraham when you get a revelation that it really does belong to you, that it is your inheritance. That is why our partners say out loud, "The Blessing of Abraham is my inheritance," **100 times every day**.

The more you speak it, the more you will believe it and the more you believe it, the more you will see it.

Romans 5:2 By whom also we have access by faith into this grace wherein we stand, and rejoice in hope of the glory of God.

The promise of The Blessing of Abraham is available by Grace and since we have access by faith into grace, we must have faith for The Blessing.

Romans 10:17 So then faith comes by hearing, and hearing by the Word of God.

Speak and Hear

God's method of increasing faith is for people to just keep speaking and hearing His Word.

Joshua 1:8 This book of the law shall not depart out of thy mouth, but you shall meditate (speak, utter) therein day and night, that thou may observe to do according to all that is written therein: for then thou shall make thy way prosperous, and then thou shall have good success.

God wants His Word in the mouths of His people because faith comes by hearing and <u>when you speak God's Word, you hear God's Word</u>.

The secret to receiving from God is to find His promise and speak it Word for Word, over and over and over, until you receive it. This may take days, or weeks, or months, but it works every time. Abraham called himself, "Father of many people," for only 3 months, and his **90 year old wife** got pregnant and had a bouncing baby boy.

You speak God's Word out loud <u>100 times per day,</u> concerning The Blessing of Abraham, or any other promise of God, for 3 months, and see what happens to you. Your whole life will change.

> **Isaiah 51:16 And <u>I have put My words in thy mouth</u>, and I have covered thee in the shadow of My hand, that I may plant the heavens, and lay the foundations of the earth, and say unto Zion, Thou art My people.**

God knows that if His Word is in your mouth, it will produce faith.

If you get a revelation of how Abraham connected to The Blessing in faith, you can do the same thing. Abraham called things, "That be not," as though they were. You can and should do the same thing.

Confess God's Word concerning what you want or need even if you do not believe it. You will. Abraham did not believe God's Word that he was going to be a father of many people when he started calling himself by his new name, Abraham, which means father of many people. His life soon changed because he was now speaking the same Words that God spoke concerning his situation. If you speak God's Word out loud, concerning your situation, your life will also change.

> **Genesis 17:4-5 As for me, behold, my covenant is with thee, and thou shall be a father of many people. ⁵ Neither shall thy name any more be called Abram, but thy name shall be Abraham (father of many people); for a father of many people have I made thee.**

> **Romans 4:17 (As it is written, I have made thee a father of many nations,) before him whom he believed, even God, who quickens the dead, and calls those things which be not as though they were.**

God Called Abraham, father of many people. Finally, Abraham called himself father of many people by speaking his own name and when he believed what he was saying, it happened. If you called yourself Blessed and really believed it, you would be Blessed. Call yourself Blessed, **until you believe it,** and then you will have it.

Do not be deceived by how simple this is.

Abraham was obedient to leave home when God called him, but he walked in the Blessing as his faith grew for it and so will everyone else.

Abraham called himself Blessed and became Blessed. I call myself Blessed, over and over, all day, every day and I am becoming Blessed just like Abraham.

Abraham's faith became so strong, that he believed that he would become a father of many people through Isaac, even if he sacrificed him, because God would just raise him up. That is some powerful faith.

Hebrews 11:11 Through faith also Sarah herself received strength to conceive seed, and was delivered of a child when she was past age, because she judged Him faithful who had promised.

Because Sarah judged God faithful to perform the Word He had spoken to them; her body became young, beautiful and strong enough to have a baby at the age of 90. **Sarah was so beautiful at the age of 90,** that King Abimelech snatched her away for his harem. **What's up with that? Are any of you ladies interested in having The Blessing?** That is also some powerful faith, but it is only an example of what faith can do. Faith in The Blessing of Abraham overrides time, nature and your age.

Romans 4:19-21 And being not weak in faith, he considered not his own body now dead, when he was about an hundred years old, neither yet the deadness of Sarah's womb: [20] He staggered not at the promise of God through unbelief; but was strong in faith, giving glory to God; [21] And being fully persuaded that, what God had promised, he was able also to perform.

Genesis 25:1-2 Then again Abraham took a wife, and her name was Keturah.[2] And she bare him Zimran, and Jokshan, and Medan, and Midian, and Ishbak, and Shuah.

Abraham was too old at the age of 100 to father children. When he developed faith for The Blessing, he was still fathering children (six more) at the age of 137 with his new wife. He watched this new family grow up and he lived another 38 years. **HELLO**. Are any of you men interested in having The Blessing?‽

You can only hear something a certain number of times before you will believe it. Politicians know this. That is why they will spend billions of dollars during every election. They are running television and radio advertisements, trying to convince you that they are wonderful, that they have the right ideas and that their opponents are not good people and have bad ideas.

The Communists used to employ a technique to get people to think differently. They called it **re-education**, we called it **brain washing**. They would sit a person in a room and have someone tell them the same thing, over and over, for weeks or months, until they believed it and there was no longer any doubt. Use the same technique to increase your faith for The Blessing of Abraham.

<u>**Speak God's Word out loud,**</u> over and over, for weeks or months, until all traces of doubt are gone. You will develop your faith to the point where The Fullness of The Blessing will be operating in all areas of your life. Use the water of God's Word to wash your brain and your faith will grow.

Or, you could take me home with you and I will sit in front of you, all day long every day, and loudly say, "The Blessing of Abraham is your inheritance and it belongs to you." You will eventually receive The Blessing.

I am going to let you in on a **huge secret**. Have you ever wondered why, or how, people like Kenneth Copeland, Keith Moore, Creflo Dollar, Charles Capps and others receive from God? I am going to tell you how they do it. Then you can do the same thing to increase your faith, for The Blessing of Abraham or anything else.

If your **determination factor** is as high as theirs is, you can do this and get the same results, concerning The Blessing of Abraham, healing, or anything else. **If you want to be successful, do what successful people do.**

They will set aside as much time as they need and **"Feed their spirits"** on God's Word, concerning what they want or need at the time. They will read every verse they can find on that subject, out loud, over and over. They listen to good preaching about that same subject and then confess God's Word on the same subject, over and over, until their faith increases.

They always receive what they want or need, whether it is The Blessing of Abraham, healing, or anything else. They will do this for days, weeks, or months, whatever it takes. They know it is God's will for them to have it and they will not quit until they get it.

It is the same method as the **Total Immersion Technique,** which our government uses to teach a new language to people so that they can work as language interpreters.

If you cannot set aside a week or a month, then use the **Partial Immersion Technique where you set aside a certain period of time each day and immerse yourself in God's Word concerning The Blessing or whatever else you need. This absolutely works, so do it if you want the Blessing of Abraham to operate in your life.**

God said in His word, that the Blessing of Abraham is our inheritance and if we will just say the same thing and believe it, we will walk in it. **Just say it until you believe it. How simple is this???**

Galatians 3:29 And if ye be Christ's, then are ye Abraham's seed, and heirs according to the promise.

Pray God's Word back to Him

When you keep saying the same thing that God said, until you believe it, it will happen in your life.

The Blessing of Abraham is something that comes upon you, but it must be inside of you first. The more of God's Word concerning The Blessing that you get inside of you, the more The Blessing will work in your life.

Confession is saying the same thing that God said. Jesus is the High Priest of our confession, which means, that the minute you confess God's Word and believe it, Jesus will make it happen.

Hebrews 3:1 Wherefore, holy brethren, partakers of the heavenly calling, consider the Apostle and High Priest of our confession, Christ Jesus;

Hebrews 4:14 Seeing then that we have a great high priest, that is passed into the heavens, Jesus the Son of God, let us hold fast our confession.

Hebrews 10:23 Let us hold fast the confession of our faith without wavering; (for he is faithful that promised;)

Keep speaking God's Word until your faith for The Blessing grows to the point where you are walking in the fullness of it.

Say out loud, "The Blessing of Abraham is my inheritance. I am called to inherit the Blessing. I know it belongs to me. I have The Blessing and I am Blessed."

Share this book with everyone you know who needs to increase their faith for The Blessing.

Chapter 6

THE THRONE OF GRACE

Knowledge Creates Boldness to Approach God

Isaiah 6:1-4 In the year that king Uzziah died I saw also the LORD sitting upon a <u>Throne</u>, high and lifted up, and his train filled the temple.

²Above it stood the seraphims: each one had six wings; with two he covered his face, and with two he covered his feet, and with two he did fly.

³ And one cried unto another, and said, Holy, holy, holy, is the LORD of hosts: the whole earth is full of his glory.

⁴ And the posts of the door moved at the voice of him that cried, and the house was filled with smoke.

Hebrews 4:16 Let us therefore come <u>Boldly</u> unto the <u>Throne of Grace</u>, that we may obtain mercy, and find grace to help in time of need.

At the cross, Jesus paid for our total redemption.

Now all we need to do is to walk boldly into the Throne of Grace and receive what has already been paid for.

There is a pathway that leads from the cross to the Throne of Grace and it is marked Redemption.

Most Christians spend their whole lives at the cross, or the area in between the cross and the Throne of Grace, which is the wilderness. It is not bondage, but it is not the Promised Land either. People in the wilderness have what Joyce Meyer calls a "Wilderness mentality," or what Keith Moore calls a "Poverty mentality."

The Curse of The Law is in full operation in the wilderness. People living there are experiencing a hard life, full of sickness and poverty. God's people are not supposed to live this way.

Walk into the Throne of Grace with your receipt, marked paid in full, which is The Word of God, and expect to receive The Blessing of Abraham

Isaiah 43:26 Put me in remembrance: let us plead together: declare thou, that you may be justified.

When you put God in remembrance, what you should be reminding Him of is what He said in His Word.

Revelation Knowledge of God's Word, creates boldness.

Go in Boldly and tell God about your Qualifications for The Blessing.

When you decide to ask God for the Grace to walk in the Fullness of His Blessing, come boldly into the Throne of Grace. Walk past the 24 Elders and all of the six-winged Seraphims and Say, "Hello Father God, it's me again. I am here to get Grace for The Blessing that You promised Father Abraham and his heirs and that is me. I am a child of Abraham and heir according to the promise, which is the Blessing. I know that The Blessing of Abraham belongs to me."

Grace, which is God's ability and favor for The Blessing of Abraham is in the Throne Room with your name on it, already paid for. Now go in boldly and get it and take your receipt with you, which is covered with The Blood of Jesus.

Deuteronomy 28:8 The LORD shall command the blessing upon thee in thy storehouses, and in all that thou sets your hand unto; and he shall bless thee in the land which the LORD thy God give thee.

Also take your Bible into the Throne of Grace with you. Make your case to The Lord for why you should have Grace to live in The Blessing of Abraham. Give God the verses to back up your claim.

The more often you come boldly into The Throne of Grace and completely state your case, the stronger your faith will become. Keep going in day after day, week after week, month after month until you are living in the fullness of The Blessing of Abraham like you are suppose to.

Several years ago I had a kidney stone, which started at 7 AM while I was preparing food for a dinner party, which was to take place that evening. I was in excruciating pain. I went into The Throne of Grace and said, "Lord, Your Word says, that by the stripes of Jesus I was healed. Now You heal me." Nothing happened. I did this all day long, even standing on the couch and holding up my Bible, so the Lord could see it better. I would say, "Do you see this Lord? Your Word says that by the stripes of Jesus I was healed; now You heal me."

I kept it up and got louder and louder. Mary left the house because it became just too intense for her. Finally, at 2 PM The Lord spoke to me in an audible voice inside my belly and said "I am going to heal you. Go to the dinner party tonight and there will be a lady there (he showed me a picture of her in my mind). Have her pray for you and I will heal you." I said, "Thank You Lord." When I got to the party that night I ask the lady to pray for me, just as The Lord had directed. The pain immediately began to subside and in less than an hour I was completely healed.

When you come into The Throne of Grace, and your <u>determination factor</u> is high, you are going to get what you came for every time.

People with no faith will beg God for what they want or need and receive nothing. They will even have all of their friends pray for them. Some of them will activate "Prayer chains" and get no results. If you need something, find one person who will pray the prayer of faith over you and you will receive every time.

People who have great faith will make a demand on God's Word and receive every time.

State your case.

When my son was little he would come and sit by me on the couch and say, "Dad, don't talk, just listen." He would then state his case for why he should get what he wanted. He would say, "I did my homework, cleaned my room, took the dog out, ate all of my dinner and practiced my baseball. Now you should take me to the store and get me what I want." I always did.

You State Your Case to God At The Throne of Grace

Say, "Lord, I am born again and therefore I am the seed of Abraham. Paul said, 'I am an heir of the promise,' which is The Blessing. I know the Blessing of Abraham is already mine."

Galatians 3:29 And if ye be Christ's, then are ye Abraham's seed, and heirs according to the promise.

Hebrews 6:13-14 For when God made promise to Abraham, because he could swear by no greater, he swore by himself, [14] Saying, Surely blessing I will bless thee, and multiplying I will multiply thee

Say, "Lord, I know the promise that You made to Abraham is The Blessing and it is my inheritance. As a matter of fact, Peter even said I am called to inherit The Blessing."

1 Peter 3:9 Not rendering evil for evil, or railing for railing: but contrariwise blessing; knowing that ye are thereunto called, that you should Inherit The Blessing.

Say, "Lord, The Blessing has been **voice activated** in my life. I have had The Blessing spoken over me by someone in authority to do so. This person has faith to speak over me. I have spoken The Blessing over myself and I believe that what I say will come to pass."

Genesis 14:18-20 And Melchizedek king of Salem brought forth bread and wine: and he was the priest of the most high God. [19] And he blessed him, and said, Blessed be Abram of the most high God, possessor of heaven and earth: [20] And blessed be the most high God, which hath delivered your enemies into thy hand. And he gave him tithes of all.

Say, "Lord, I tithe and I know that because of that, You will open the windows of Heaven and pour me out a Blessing that there shall not be enough room to receive it. And Lord, I know that You are talking about The Garden of Eden Blessing."

Malachi 3:10 Bring ye all the tithes into the storehouse, that there may be meat in mine house, and prove me now herewith, said the LORD of hosts, if I will not open you the windows of heaven, and pour you out a blessing, that there shall not be room enough to receive it.

Say, "Lord, I am Blessed because I trust in You alone to provide for me."

Jeremiah 17:7 Blessed is the man that trusts in the LORD, and whose hope the LORD is.

Say, "Lord, Jesus has redeemed me from the Curse of The Law so that The Blessing of Abraham can come on me."

Galatians 3:13-14 Christ hath redeemed us from the curse of the law, being made a curse for us: for it is written, Cursed is every one that hangs on a tree: ¹⁴ That the blessing of Abraham might come on the Gentiles through Jesus Christ; that we might receive the promise of the Spirit through faith.

Say, "Lord, I have commanded The Curse of The Law, and the devil that has been causing it to operate in my life, to leave me in the Name of Jesus."

Mark 16:17 And these signs shall follow them that believe; In my name shall they cast out devils; they shall speak with new tongues.

Say, "Lord, I hearken to and obey the voice of Your Word, so The Blessing of Abraham is supposed to come on me and overtake me."

Deuteronomy 28:2 And all these Blessings shall come on thee, and overtake thee, if thou shall hearken unto the voice of the LORD thy God.

Say, "Lord, I deserve to receive The Blessing of Abraham because I am the righteousness of God by Christ Jesus and by the way, I am also supposed to be surrounded with favor."

Psalm 5:12 For You, LORD, will bless the righteous; with favor will thou surround him as with a shield.

Say, "Lord, I confess that The Blessing is mine during the day and at night."

Joshua 1:8 This book of the law shall not depart out of thy mouth; but thou shall meditate (speak) therein day and night, that thou may observe to do according to all that is written therein: for then thou shall make

thy way prosperous, and then thou shall have good success.

I can absolutely tell you, <u>from a very personal experience</u>, that The Throne of Grace, in Heaven, is a real place. Our Wonderful Heavenly Father, The creator of the universe, The Great I Am, is sitting on The Throne. When you boldly come in, you have <u>His undivided attention</u>.

The more revelation knowledge you have of God's Word, the bolder you will be when you come into The Throne of Grace. You have a right to be there because the King who sits on the Throne is your Father. You are his child, you are royalty. He loves you. He loves to see you in person. He loves the sound of your voice when you talk to Him. **He will give you Grace to walk in the Fullness of The Blessing of Abraham.**

Say out loud, "Father God, I am here to receive Grace for Your Blessing. I know I have The Blessing of Abraham because Your Word says it belongs to me and it is my inheritance. I thank you for it right now in the wonderful name of Your Dear Son, Jesus."

If you think this book is important to the body of Christ, send everyone you know an E-mail and tell them about it.

167
SCRIPTURAL

Facts About The Blessing

1. Every church should be getting people saved, filled with the Holy Spirit and Blessed with the Blessing of Abraham.

2. If people knew they could receive the fullness of The Blessing of God at church, they would be knocking down the doors and tearing holes in the roof to get in.

3. There are two things every born again Christian must know to live a successful life in the Kingdom of God. What God has given to us, and how to possess it.

4. Living in the Garden of Eden with The Blessing, is God's perfect will for His people.

5. The Garden of Eden is still where God desires for his people to live.

6. If you are living without the fullness of the Blessing of God, you are not living your life according to the will of God.

7. People who have the Blessing will find that success comes easy in everything they do. People who do not have The Blessing will struggle just to achieve moderate success and will eventually lose most of what they do earn.

8. Pay no attention to adverse situations or circumstances **because nothing else matters but The Blessing.**

9. If you are not living in The Blessing of Abraham, the curse will operate in your life. Read Deut. 28:15-68 if any of this is going on in your life, blame the curse.

10. Jesus came that we might have life and to have it more abundantly. Anything less should never be acceptable.

11. The Body of Christ is meant to live in The Blessing of Abraham.

12. A major purpose of The Blessing of God is to enable us to be a Blessing to others.

13. The Blessing of God puts up a wall around you that the curse cannot get through. Job 1:10

14. Speaking fear will cause the Blessing wall to come down and allow the devil to get in. Job 3:25

15. God said The Blessing is not subject to change because He confirmed it with an oath, which He swore by Himself. Hebrews 6:13-18

16. It is just as much God's will to Bless you today as it was when He spoke The Blessing over Adam, Noah, Abraham, Isaac, Jacob and Joseph.

17. You can use the name of Jesus to enforce The Blessing.

18. You should believe you have The Blessing of Abraham because you do. Now all you need is the faith to have it operating in your life.

19. You will become like the people you are listening to and eventually you will have what they have. Make sure you are listening to people who have The Blessing of Abraham. Do not listen to unsaved people who are living with sickness, poverty and sin.

20. We are called to be distributors of The Blessing to others.

21. At the time that you were born again, you <u>were</u> redeemed and Blessed with The Blessing of Abraham which means that you already have The Blessing. Gal. 3:9. Now all you need to do is learn how to possess it.

22. The Blessing of Abraham belongs to you because you are an heir of the Promise. Gal. 3:29 The Blessing of Abraham is <u>your inheritance</u>.

23. A person planted by the water is a person connected to The Blessing of Abraham and that is me. How about you?

24. God Blessed Adam, Noah, Abraham, Isaac, Jacob, Joseph and you and me with exactly the same Blessing, with the same purpose.

25. The original purpose of the Blessing that God spoke over Adam in the Garden of Eden was to expand the Garden and that purpose for The Blessing has never changed.

26. The Blessing of God will create and expand a Garden of Eden in the life of anyone it comes upon, because that is its purpose.

27. When you live in the Blessing of Abraham sickness and poverty must leave, because they do not belong in the Garden of Eden.

28. When The Blessing of God comes upon you, the area you have authority over will become your Garden of Eden and will affect your whole family, business and everything you have jurisdiction over.

29. Every place in the Bible that mentions God, or Jesus, or anyone Blessing anyone, the purpose of The Blessing that they spoke, was to empower for success, and to create and expand the Garden of Eden.

30. The Blessing of Abraham is meant to change the wilderness into the Garden of Eden and it does just that. Isaiah 51:1-3

31. When Abraham was Blessed by God he became Possessor of Heaven and earth and also became Heir of the world and we are Abraham's heirs, so what does that tell you? Genesis 14:19 and Romans 4:13

32. We are heirs according to the promise and the promise was The Blessing of Abraham. Gal. 3:29 & Hebrews 6:13

33. Jesus said in John 3:27 "A man can be given nothing unless it is given to him from Heaven." We have already been given The Blessing of Abraham, from God in Heaven. Galatians 3:9

34. Jesus Blessed the two fishes and five loaves and they multiplied into enough food to feed five thousand people, because when anything is Blessed, it multiplies. Be careful when you Bless your food.

35. God Blessed Sarah and her body became young and beautiful. She also multiplied into a great nation of people, because of The Blessing.

36. The Blessing, God was talking about in Malachi 3:10, is the Garden of Eden Blessing and when God opens the windows of Heaven and pours it out, there is not enough room to receive it.

37. Because of the covenant with Abraham, which is The Blessing, God gives us power to get wealth. Deut. 8:18. I'm OK with that.

38. The Blessing of Abraham brings health, prosperity, victory, dominion, peace, power to be a Blessing and everything else you will ever need or desire.

39. Psalms 23 is written by David who was talking about the Blessing of Abraham Life. "My cup runs over" is the Blessing of Abraham in operation the way it is meant to be in your life also.

40. Faith <u>in</u> The Blessing of Abraham will release it to work in your life.

41. Be bold to receive the Blessing of Abraham because it already belongs to you. Gal.3:9

42. The minute that you get a revelation that the Blessing of Abraham belongs to you, your life will begin to change. Ours did.

43. The Blessing of God is the solution for any problem you might ever have.

44. Become Blessing minded. See yourself as The Blessed of God.

45. You must believe that The Blessing of Abraham has the power to do what it is intended to do. That is to create and expand the Garden of Eden in the life of anyone who has faith for it.

46. The Blessing of Abraham cannot operate in your life until the Curse of The Law has been removed.

47. The Blessing and the curse cannot both exist in the same area of your life, at the same time. It would be like trying to fill a glass with water and air at the same time.

48. Isaac became very rich during a famine because he had faith for The Blessing of Abraham. Genesis 26.

49. The state of the economy or adverse political circumstances cannot stop or affect the Blessing of Abraham.

50. The Blessing of Abraham just creates the Garden of Eden wherever it goes and takes no circumstances, or situations into consideration.

51. The Blessing of Abraham will create A Garden of Eden in your life and cause you to live the abundant life that Jesus came to provide for you.

52. The Blessing of Abraham works 24 hours a day.

53. Pastors and Priests are <u>commanded by God</u> to speak The Blessing over the people, <u>word for word</u>. Numbers 6:22-27

54. People who have authority to speak The Blessing of Abraham over you are your Parents, your Pastor, Priest, Rabbi, or any Minister of God's Word that you financially support. Gen. 27 & 28, Numbers 6 and Philippians 4:19

55. If you will receive The Blessing when it is spoken over you, by a person in authority to do so, you will live in the Blessing of God.

56. When I speak The Blessing over the people in my church, or my partners, I intend for the Blessing of Abraham, the Garden of Eden Blessing, to come into their lives.

57. We have had many people actually receive The Blessing that I spoke over them. Two of them became millionaires in very short order. Others received huge financial increase as well as healings. Who wants to be the next person to have The Blessing of Abraham spoken over them?

58. The Jews are the most financially blessed group of people in the world because they speak Blessings over their children on a regular basis, and the Rabbi speaks The Blessing over all of them. They understand and have faith for and in the Blessing of Abraham.

59. The level of The Blessing you are willing to settle for is the highest level of The Blessing you will ever reach. You should not settle for anything less than the fullness of The Blessing of Abraham.

60. When God spoke The Blessing over Adam, The Blessing was all in one piece.

61. Sin broke up The Blessing into little pieces which have been called "elements" of The Blessing.

62. There is a big difference between everyday blessings and "The Blessing of Abraham."

63. People many times think they are Blessed of The Lord when they get any blessing, like a healing, or money to pay the rent. Compared to what is available to you, in the actual Blessing of Abraham, those are small blessings.

64. Many Christians are poor because they do not know how to increase their faith for The Blessing of Abraham, or that it is even available to them.

65. Don't believe for **a** blessing; believe for **The** Blessing of Abraham.

66. Don't desire to be rich, desire The Blessing of Abraham.

67. If you are a son or daughter of Abraham you are an heir to the promise, which is The Blessing of Abraham and you have a right to live in it. Gal. 3:29 The Blessing is your **birthright**.

68. The way God treated Abraham, Isaac, Jacob and Joseph under the Blessing of Abraham, is the same way He will treat us under The Blessing of Abraham.

69. There is no such thing as The Blessing of Abraham apart from Jesus, because it came through Him. He redeemed us and qualified us for it.

70. Stay close to people who have The Blessing of Abraham and you will also be Blessed and then don't leave them. Ask Lot how that works.

71. When The Blessing of the Lord comes on a person they know it right away. It's like being filled with The Holy Spirit. You know when you get it. You begin to think different.

72. The Blessing of Abraham will change your surroundings.

73. The Lord will Bless the righteous and surround them with favor. When you are Blessed of God you also have favor. Ps 5:12

74. If you are waiting for God to Bless you, you may wait a long time.

75. Pray the prayer of Jabez. If God gave Jabez the Blessing, He will give it to you because you have a better covenant.

76. When you decide to ask God for Grace to live in the Fullness of His Blessing, come boldly into the Throne of Grace. Walk past the 24 Elders and all of the six-winged Seraphims and Say, "Hello Father God, it's me again. I am here to get Grace for The Blessing that You promised Abraham and his heirs

and that is me. I am a child of Abraham and heir according to the promise, which is the Blessing."

77. Tell Father God (state your case) why you should have Grace for The Blessing of Abraham. You are His child, He is your father, He loves you and you belong in there. Hebrews 4:16 Isaiah 43:26 Say, "I am righteous, redeemed, and a covenant person, and The Blessing already belongs to me. Thank you."

78. Do not ask for The Blessing, it already belongs to you. Ask God to manifest it in your life and then declare that you have it, until you get it.

79. God wants you to have the fullness of The Blessing of Abraham. Anything else you hear, or think, **is wrong**.

80. When you hearken (hear and declare) unto the voice of The Lord, and do all of His commandments, The Blessing of Abraham will overtake you.

81. Jesus has redeemed us from the curse of the law and made us qualified for The Blessing.

82. The Gospel God preached to Abraham, was that the Blessing would come to all people of the earth, through him.

83. If you are righteous, and you are if you are born again, you deserve to be Blessed because of what Jesus did for you. Not because of anything you did.

84. We need to lay hold (receive, take) of The Blessing, just like we do with eternal life. 1 Timothy 6:12

85. We live in The Blessing of Abraham through faith, because it is impossible to receive anything from God, without faith. Hebrews 11:6

86. The measure of The Blessing we live in is according to our faith. Matthew 9:29.

87. The Tithe is The Blessing connector.

88. You cannot earn The Blessing.

89. You cannot work your way into The Blessing.

90. Obedience does not always bring The Blessing, although disobedience can stop The Blessing.

91. God did not pick Kenneth Copeland to have The Blessing, although he did pick him to teach and anointed him. Brother Copeland lives in the Blessing of Abraham, by faith, just like Abraham did.

92. We must develop faith in the Power and ability of The Blessing.

93. A Blessed person may not do everything right, but they are empowered to succeed.

94. When your children have been Blessed, they are empowered to succeed and they will.

95. Famines and economic recessions mean nothing to The Blessing.

96. The Blessing is a huge part of the Gospel.

97. Your Words will bring The Blessing into your life, when they are spoken in faith.

98. You can receive The Blessing by praying the Prayer of Faith, which is asking in faith, nothing wavering, believing that you receive when you ask. Mark 11:24

99. When you confess God's Word long enough concerning The Blessing, you will have it. Just keep saying, "I believe I have The Blessing" until you receive it.

100. God Blesses you through His Word, but His Word must be spoken. Speaking The Word of God, on The Blessing, brings The Blessing.

101. Everything God Promised to Abraham belongs to us.

102. Use the Total Immersion Technique (immersing yourself in God's Word concerning The Blessing) to get The Blessing. It takes a certain amount of hours for this to work and it varies from one person to another.

103. The Blessing of Abraham on you will make people around you rich, like Lot for example.

104. Become totally committed to living in The Blessing. Everything is a matter of priorities. The Blessing of God should be **VERY HIGH** on your list. If someone is teaching about The Blessing, BE THERE!

105. When you get excited about The Blessing you are getting close to living in The Blessing.

106. The Blessing is a process but it can happen very quickly.

107. Asking God for faith to receive The Blessing is a waste of your time and His.

108. Faith for The Blessing only comes by hearing the Word of God about The Blessing.

109. God is not looking for people with money; He is looking for people who want The Blessing.

110. Abraham called himself <u>Father of Nations</u> for three months and then his ninety year old wife became pregnant. How long are you willing to call yourself <u>Blessed of the Lord</u> to get yourself Blessed of the Lord?

111. God's Word is the seed that produces faith. Mark 4:14

112. Confess, "I believe I have The Blessing of the Lord," until you have it. Say it until you believe it and then you will have it. If you hear anything enough times you will eventually believe it.

113. Hearing God's Word, on The Blessing of God, produces faith. So you should listen, every chance you get, to God's Word on The Blessing of Abraham.

114. God has already given us The Blessing. We just need the faith to receive it and possess it. Gal. 3:9

115. When you come to the point where you understand that your faith is not as strong as it needs to be, to live in The Blessing of Abraham, you become empowered to increase your faith by listening to God's Word.

116. Don't try to stand on faith, for The Blessing that you do not have. Many people die and go broke standing on faith they do not have.

117. People who believe that, "God is going to Bless us some day," never seem to get it. That used to be us.

118. Never oppose or say anything bad, about a Blessed person.

119. When you have The Fullness of The Blessing of Abraham, everyone will know it.

120. The Blessing will produce everything you will ever want or need.

121. The Blessing overcomes all obstacles in a person's life.

122. Failure for anyone to live in The Blessing of Abraham is never God's fault. It is always a faith issue.

123. The Blessing is our inheritance from our Father Abraham.

124. Fear contaminates Faith for the Blessing of God.

125. Un-forgiveness also contaminates faith for The Blessing.

126. Walking in love keeps us in the brightness of The Blessing of God.

127. When you combine The Blessing of Abraham with smart business people you get John D. Rockefeller, The man who owns Chick-fil-A, the Hobby Lobby Guy and most of the Jewish people.

128. You do not even need to be smart, well educated or good looking (like me) to be highly successful if you are living in the Blessing of Abraham.

129. Nothing else matters but The Blessing of Abraham, when it comes to being successful.

130. Learn to trust the Blessing of Abraham to provide for you.

131. Let The Blessing work for you.

132. The Blessing of Abraham will cause everything you have ever lost, or had stolen from you, to quickly come back to you. Luke 18:8

133. The Blessing of Abraham causes the angels to work for you.

134. The Blessing of Abraham is a material Blessing. God likes material things, like streets of gold, for example.

135. Seeking the Kingdom of God first is seeking the Blessing of God.

136. Living in the Kingdom of God is living in the Blessing of God.

137. You cannot live a successful life in the Kingdom of God without The Blessing of Abraham.

138. You cannot dominate your area of authority, or rule and reign in this life, without The Blessing of Abraham.

139. The Blessing of the Lord makes a person rich and He adds no sorrow (toil, hard work) to it. <u>If you want to stay poor, do not ask God for the Blessing</u>.

140. When a person is Blessed of The Lord, they and their children will increase.

141. When a person is Blessed of the Lord, wealth and riches are in their house.

142. When a person is Blessed of the Lord, favor surrounds them like a shield.

143. When a person is Blessed of the Lord, everything they do prospers.

144. The Lord commands The Blessing upon you in your storehouses.

145. The Blessing that is poured out from the open windows of Heaven, for people who tithe, is the Garden of Eden Blessing.

146. The Blessing of Abraham trumps a bad economy.

147. The entire country of Egypt lived in abundance during a famine because the Blessing of Abraham was on Joseph.

148. The Blessing of God released the dream of Joseph.

149. Do not attempt to start a business or a ministry without first receiving The Blessing of Abraham.

150. The Blessing will greatly expand your area of influence. People will listen to you because they will want to know where you got what you have.

151. There is a Garden of Eden Covenant. Isaiah 51:3

152. You can be born again and filled with the Holy Spirit and still have the curse of the law operating in different areas of your life, such as your health and finances.

153. If you have health problems or financial problems, you should always blame The Curse of The Law. Deuteronomy 28:15-68

154. Tithing will turn off the curse switch in your finances.

155. The curse is the exact opposite of The Blessing.

156. If you are not prospering in your ways, the curse is operating in your life.

157. If you are experiencing any lack of anything, the curse is operating in your life.

158. If you are experiencing sickness of any type, the curse is operating in your life.

159. Any operation of the curse in your life is considered to be double jeopardy. The curse is the penalty for sin and Jesus paid the penalty for poverty by becoming poor, for sickness by His stripes and for sin by His blood and His life. You do not need to pay for sin, Jesus did.

160. Do not let the devil make you pay the penalty that has already been paid. Jesus does not need your help to pay for our sins. "It is finished".

161. When you are living in The Blessing by faith, a wall goes up around you and the curse of the law can no longer operate in your life.

162. When you have faith for The Blessing of Abraham, your domain (area of authority) becomes a Garden of Eden and will constantly expand.

163. When the fullness of The Blessing of Abraham comes into your life, sickness, poverty and strife must leave, as anything bad cannot stay.

164. When The Blessing of Abraham comes upon you, your house is filled with love, peace and joy.

165. The Bible is The Blessing Book. Read Gal. 3:7, 9, 13, 14, 29 out loud every day.

166. If you seek The Blessing of Abraham with all of your heart, you will live in the fullness of it.

Say out loud, "I have inherited The Blessing of Abraham, through Jesus, and I believe I receive it right now."

Tell all of your Facebook friends about this book so they can also live in The Blessing.

If you have a twitter account, tweet everyone you know, and tell them about this book.

ABOUT THE AUTHOR

Pastor Jim Kibler was born in Pittsburgh and grew up in Slippery Rock, Pennsylvania. He is a graduate of Mount St. Mary's College in Emmitsburg, Maryland and Rhema Bible College in Tulsa, Oklahoma. He also did graduate work in business at George Washington University in Washington DC. He is Pastor of Victory Christian Chapel, in Melbourne, Florida.

Pastor Jim's popular website is **www.increasenow.com**, a free site, where people around the world listen to his messages on God's Goodness, Redemption and The Blessing.

Pastor Jim and his wife Mary, who is also a graduate of Rhema Bible College, host the popular radio program, Increase Now, on The Word of Faith Radio Network.

In addition, Pastor Jim is a Very Entertaining, Financial Increase and Motivational Conference Speaker and everywhere he speaks, finances increase and churches grow. He makes God's Word very easy to understand.

Pastor Jim may be contacted at jkibler100@aol.com.

Other Books by Pastor Jim:

If the Bible Is True

The Blessing and The Tithe

ABOUT THE AUTHOR

THE BLESSING

ABOUT THE AUTHOR

THE BLESSING

Made in the USA
Middletown, DE
11 September 2021